Success: For Minority Teens (& Their Friends)

What does it take to be successful...Really?

By C. Osvaldo Gomez
(Homie G)

Printed in the United States of America

ISBN: 9781521575932
Imprint: Independently published at Amazon.com

Contents

You're Born A Lamborghini, But You Live
Like A Bucket

Dedication

This book is dedicated to the thousands of students I have had the pleasure of teaching, knowing, and learning from. You have filled my life with purpose, and for that I am eternally grateful.

Acknowledgement

This book wouldn't have been possible without the support of various friends and former co-workers throughout my years as an educator. Most notably, I'd like to thank retired high school Principal, Varda Levy, for using her English teacher background to go through these chapters and point out where I needed clarity and casual language. I'd also like to thank her for offering me words of encouragement throughout the process. Thanks, Varda! Gal Gadot has nothing on you!

Next, I'd like to thank current high school Principal, Marcela Miranda (also a former English teacher), for helping me with chapter formatting and making the book more engaging. Thank you also for your valuable insight on how skin color among Latinx students factors heavily on how they are perceived and treated by non-Latinx educators. Keep making a difference, *pequebou!*

I want to also acknowledge, Diana Quiroga, Los Angeles Unified School District administrator for making connections between what I wrote and her understanding of the concept of "grit." She made some valid points that got me thinking and writing.

While writing this book I got discouraged a few times, but one individual helped me get back on the laptop: my wife, Jessica Grimmett-Gomez. She also encouraged me to keep making helpful YouTube videos for teens on my channel, Teacher Homie G.

I want to thank my parents, Carlos and Teresa Gomez for being consistent with me as a child and stressing the importance of education to me in their own unique ways. My dad took me to work as a young man plenty of times and from this I learned that getting an education was my ticket out of a future of hard physical labor and low pay. My mom made sure I was fed well before school and after school, and was always openly worrying about me coming home safely every time I left the house. I never wanted to do anything stupid to disappoint her.

My *Encuentros* Leadership elective students were also instrumental in helping to make this book happen. They were willing to listen to and read book chapters, telling me where I needed to make the book "less boring" and what sections they enjoyed reading the most. This helped me gauge where I needed to do some revisions. Thanks, little homies!

Finally, I'd like to thank all of the students that I have worked with over the last 16 years as both a teacher and assistant principal. You motivate me to be my best and give you all I have to offer. My life has way more meaning because of you. This book is how I can repay you and future students.

Foreword

Let's talk about the title of this book. The story begins at least two years ago, when I made the decision to one day write a book on the topic of success whose target audience would be minority teens (students of color). Amazon, of course, was one of the first places I looked online for representative book samples. Not surprisingly, most of the books on success for teens were written for ALL teens and by white authors. Nothing wrong with this, obviously. I just felt in my heart that minority teens, especially those that are not avid readers, would perhaps like to read about success from authors with similar backgrounds and/or experiences.

Now I don't pretend to know what it means to be African American, American Indian, Vietnamese, Samoan, Chinese, etc. Every ethnic group in this country has a unique signature with respect to their cultures and values. Luckily, my experience as a teacher in the Bay Area and in Southern California has given me ample proof that although there are vast differences among minority teens, they do share a common bond around their struggles with race, poverty, identity, authority, and assimilation, within our school system. With much respect for all minority groups in this country, I ask that you excuse my use of "…For Minority Teens…" in the title of this book.

I've never liked excluding others in anything associated with me. Although I set out with a mission of completing a book on success specifically to address the unique needs of minority students, I discovered as I wrote that many of the life lessons I share apply to teenagers across all ethnic lines. There is plenty of application in the suggestions and exercises to be of help to all teens, meaning, also all of my little, non-minority *homies.* In fact, many of the people who reviewed this book insisted that I add something in the title to include non-minority teens, seeing plenty of relevance in the text for them. This is why the title also includes the words, "(& Their Friends)."

Finally, I want to talk about the main question this book tries to answer, i.e., the subtitle: *What does it take to be successful...Really?* Success means so many different things to everyone. I've read at least 50 books on the topic and I've found some common themes that I used to structure each chapter here. To give the "structure" flavor and substance to teens, I used stories from my past youth or favorite movie scenes to convey powerful messages about success so young readers will be able to answer the book's question by the end of the book.

To your success,
C. Osvaldo Gomez
(Homie G)

Introduction

I spent 10 years of my life angry with white people. Every last one of them was racist. To confirm my belief about whites, I looked for racism in their words or actions, often making something out of nothing. My anger was like a beast eating me alive from within. I had to work extremely hard to keep it from tearing me apart. Only negative and destructive interactions with the *gringos* kept the beast feeling full. I distrusted every single one of them, despite what they said or did to help me. These *gringos* were my teachers.

I wasted too much energy in middle and high school being angry at the world, and taking it out on my white teachers. I was a broken kid constantly battling the past and present. My teachers spoke to me about having a bright future ahead. They tried to motivate me. To me, the future was like a soap bubble flying in the air, letting the wind take it anywhere until something in its path popped it. I was poor, an "illegal alien," a minority, a kid with an alcoholic and abusive father, and a second language learner. I had no future.

What business do I have becoming somebody? I would ask myself this question over and over. Any day I may be caught by *la migra* and get deported. My father can't stop drinking. He gets upset for any little thing I do wrong. If I'm lucky he won't hit me. If I'm lucky, he'll fall asleep on the couch and forget I exist. My sister is never home. My mother is overworked and too weak to defend me.

There's no one I can depend on. These are just a few of the many conclusions I had made back then about my situation. I had very little going for me. To make matters worse, I was suffering from both anxiety and depression, and I didn't even know it.

The future is all about uncertainty and it's why many people are scared of it. Uncertainty made my anxiety spike so I felt horribly nervous every day of my life. Depression is a deep, sometimes unexplainable sadness. It strikes without any warning. There were too many things "wrong with me" and I fell into many bouts of depression. Instead of sunny days, I always had a rain cloud over my head. Anger seemed to be the only emotion that could lift me out of the darkness and into the light.

It was anger and wanting revenge that kept me alive long enough to defeat my early challenges. It's how I got to college. If anger and revenge had been enough, I would've made it through college without any psychotic episodes. But I did not. Being away from home and my community, having to study all the time, the culture shock from attending a university (UC Santa Barbara) with mostly white students, made my demons return with their own vengeance. I felt cursed. I felt like I didn't belong there. My depression got worse. Thoughts of suicide ran through my mind all the time. I started binge drinking on the weekends to soothe my sorrow the "Mexican way."

While at a party during my first year at UCSB, a white student told me that I was only there because of Affirmative Action, a program that helped minority students get accepted. This infuriated me. He didn't know I was a junior college transfer. He didn't know I'd earned my way there by graduating from San Jose City College with a 3.66 grade point average. But he did me a favor: he revived my beast. A white woman at the Bursar's Office also kept my beast alive. I was there to pay my tuition, waiting my turn to hand over my check at the cashier's station. She came to me and asked: "Are you lost?" I said, "No." Her last question to me was, "Well, do you go to this university?" It took everything I had not to punch her in the face. She saw a buzz cut haircut, Dickies pants, an extra-large t-shirt hanging over my belt, cheap tennis shoes, and a face that didn't quite match up with the ones she'd come to expect. I had been profiled.

That lady's ignorance challenged me to prove that I belonged at UCSB. I did more than prove it. I made the Dean's List on three separate occasions and graduated with a Bachelor's of Science degree in Biological Sciences. My grade point average: 3.86.

Stop and think for a second about this: Have you ever used anger to do something positive with your life? I spent ten years working as a high school assistant principal and the students sent to my office all misused anger. They let anger get to them. They got in fights with other students or used their anger to bully others. Anger is how many of them controlled their parents! Finally, these students used anger as an excuse. "I can't help it, Homie G," they'd say to me, "I have anger issues."

This book is not an exploration on how to use anger like I did. It's going to be about how to deal with racism, problems, ignorance, pain, fear, identity, struggle, and much more. But not for the sake of making you simply feel better about yourself. The goal of this book is to take your thinking to the next level using real talk. Ultimately, my mission is to give you (and all students of color) keys to personal success no matter how *you* define success.

Unlike other books on success for teens, I'm not going to take it easy on you. I'm not here to give you validation for who you are today. I'm here to promote your constant change and this will take a hard stance on my part. You may not like my harsh tone. We don't always like what's best for us at first. In due time, we learn to appreciate how others forced us into taking notice of ourselves and of the world.

Let me give you a chapter-by-chapter overview to prepare you mentally for what is to come. After reading this book, you can always refer to this overview to remind you of each lesson and of the big picture: your success! Let's begin.

In Chapter 1, I will show you what groupthink is, and give you a better way to process racism and ignorance. The goal of the chapter is to get you to stop using racism as an excuse, to teach you how to stop being distracted by ignorance, and to show you how successful people avoid ignorance.

In Chapter 2, I will show you how to reframe your problems as opportunities. The goal of this chapter is to free you from feeling trapped by your problems so you can step out of your mental cage and keep on with your life.

In Chapter 3, I will show you how what you expect out of other people can either set you up for big disappointments or big triumphs. I'll also introduce the concept of Profitable Action to you. The goal of this chapter is to teach you the true meaning of self-reliance and to distinguish between the different types of activities you are taking (or not taking) part in.

In Chapter 4, I will show you how to write S.M.A.R.T goals that give you clear direction and control of your future. I'll also share with you the type of mindset you must possess in order to get the outcomes you desire and how to approach rejections. The goal of this chapter is to impress upon you the importance of writing out your goals, and to halt any negative attitudes you may have about outcomes and rejection.

In Chapter 5, I will show you why the majority of the people you consider to be friends at school, are really not your friends. I'll share with you how to decide who to spend time with at school or outside of school, and how to respond to "haters." The goal of this chapter is to have you think critically from now on about the people you befriend.

In Chapter 6, I will show you that how intelligent you can be isn't determined by your genetics. I'll share with you what a fixed and growth mindset are, and how to adopt a growth mindset for good. The goal of this chapter is to encourage you to keep learning, no matter how hard something gets.

In Chapter 7, I will show you how to deal with people who challenge your ethnic identity. I'll also share with you the realizations that helped me manage my own identity insecurities. The goal of this chapter is to relieve you of any guilt you may have about leaving your friends and family behind as you become more successful.

In Chapter 8, I will show you what accountability is and how to become accountable to yourself. I'll also explain how being blamed as a young person leads to a life of blame as an adult. The goal of this chapter is give you an idea of the type of personal accountability you will need to advance in life.

In Chapter 9, I will show you why most schools in America do indeed suck. I'll tell you why you can't count on them to give you an accurate evaluation of your knowledge or skills. The goal of this chapter is to convince you that your efforts are the only thing you can be sure of and to encourage you to double them.

In Chapter 10, I will show you what type of effort it takes to be successful. I'll tell you how you're severely underestimating the need to read and how much time you have in a day to be truly productive. The goal of this chapter is teach how to better manage your time with strategies successful people use to maximize their productivity.

In Chapter 11, I will show you why you must stop reading the 3 F's: fairytales, fantasies, and fiction, on your spare time. I'll explain to you why reading non-fiction books and articles is much more beneficial to your future. The goal of this chapter is to expose you to the non-fiction topics that will best prepare you for success in the 21st Century.

In Chapter 12, I will show you why it's financially foolish to start out at a four-year college after high school. I'll provide you with an inside scoop on the business side of getting a higher education degree and relate all the benefits of starting out at a junior college. The goal of this chapter is to provide you with a more affordable pathway to success.

In Chapter 13, I will show you why successful people value their health and fitness so much. I'll compare you to a Lamborghini, and explain to you why eating junk food and not exercising is treating your body like a bucket (car). The goal of this chapter is to get you to be conscious about the things that you eat and drink, and to equate success with great health.

In Chapter 14, I will show how popularity at school can transfer to success as an adult. I'll describe to you the two types of popularity somebody can have at school and introduce the concept of personal branding. The goal of this chapter is to encourage you to share more of yourself at school and to value the way you promote yourself to others.

In Chapter 15, I will introduce you to the concept of 180, where you'll work on your ability to quickly forget your poor performances and embrace having great ones again as soon as possible. The goal of this chapter is to provide you with the mindset to turn things around when you make mistakes and not allow your life lows to define you.

Enjoy!

Chapter 1

Understanding White People & Avoiding Ignorance

As a student, I used to think white people were all evil. They were out to keep me "oppressed." White people didn't want me to succeed. They wanted to keep me in my place. "The Man" was a real white person pushing buttons, and pulling levers, laughing at all us minority kids for trying to "come up" in life. I wish I had been alone in what I thought about white people because maybe I would've stopped thinking this garbage sooner. Unfortunately, the kids at my school also thought the same. This is called, groupthink.

What is groupthink? Groupthink is when a group makes wrong decisions because of peer pressure. Groupthink leads groups to ignore alternatives, other realities, and take irrational actions that put down other groups.

Even when we were in the wrong, my friends and I would have a typical response every time we got scolded in class by our teachers: "It's cuz I'm Mexican, huh?"

You know what's funny? Most of the interactions I had with white people were at school.

Your teachers are probably the only white people you know. They were the only ones I knew. Yet I had made a general conclusion about an entire ethnic group. A wrong one at that: white people are all the same.

The manager at the apartment I grew up in was white. He came by once a month to collect the rent. Month after month I saw a white man take my parent's hard earned money away. It didn't give me a good impression on white people. They were money takers to me. Sometimes my parents needed to borrow money from friends to have enough for the rent. Working as night janitors for a big corporation in Santa Clara, CA wasn't enough for them to make ends meet. My older sister and I would go hungry some days, with little to eat for dinner. I came to hate the manager of our apartment complex.

Adding to my misunderstanding of white people, our neighbors were other Mexicans, Blacks, or Vietnamese. They didn't have many nice things to say about white people either. Our common struggles as people of color needed villains. Whites were the bad guys and we were the good guys. There were a few white kids at my school, but they were poor like the rest of us, so for the most part, we all got along.

I recently read an article online about a survey conducted for the Bill and Melinda Gates Foundation. This survey reported that students of color want more teachers of color teaching them. In the study, students of color reported that they could relate better with teachers of color, suggesting they would like to have more minority teachers.

I think this study was a big waste of money and time. About the only thing it accomplished was giving those kids, the ones who participated in the study, a false sense of hope. Successful people don't hope for things to occur. I know you have been told by many people to keep your hopes up. I'm here to tell you that hope is for losers who wait to be rescued by knights in shining armor. Hope is for people who lack courage or drive to make things happen on their own. If you wait around for hope, you'll end up hopeless. Anyways, you don't need a study to prove what is already obvious—minority kids like minority teachers because we see them as our "peeps." It's been this way for decades!

One thing is to want something; another thing is determining whether or not you're actually going to get it. If I could with a flick of a wand change the teacher workforce in America so that at least 50% of all teachers were of color, I would in an instant. But I'm not a wizard. What I'm trying to say is that this is never going to happen in America. In fact, the teacher workforce in this country is going to be more ethnically white in the future. Very few minority college graduates choose teaching as a profession and I don't blame them. It's a tough job. The only thing left for you to do then is what all successful people do: accept the reality and move forward anyway. Actually, I want you take it one step further. Learn to relate to your white teachers because your white teachers are your only gateway to understanding white culture.

I didn't stop using racism as an excuse for some of my failures until after college. That was a big mistake. Trust me, faulting racism for a lack of personal accomplishments will be a big mistake for you too. Racism does exist, and it rears its ugly head sometimes, but it will do you no good to obsess about it, much like I did as a young man. You can consume hours of your life minding racism and worrying about it. Meanwhile, you are expending thousands of calories your brain could've put to better use.

Harboring stereotypes also can lead you to misjudge the intentions of many people, including whites. Often times this leads to missed opportunities for advancement and personal growth. If you're not growing as a person, and I don't mean getting taller, someone else is. Someone else will outcompete you one day for a job, a business or investing deal, or even a life partner. So focus on what's important and give racism a break from your life. Racism isn't going anywhere, right?

Learn from wealthy whites

One of the lamest myths I ever allowed to enter my mind was that only rich white folks were greedy. Television had a lot to do with it. I used to watch this cartoon called, DuckTales. It was an adventure show whose main character, Scrooge McDuck, practically killed himself for every penny he could get his hands on. "Uncle Scrooge" was filthy rich and he'd swim in a trove of gold coins and treasure almost every episode. Even though Scrooge McDuck was a duck, he represented every white man to me.

Now I know that everyone is greedy. Two major emotions all humans share are fear and greed. Yet in my mind I couldn't be greedy and neither could my homies at school or anyone one at my school for that matter. We're kids from "the hood," I thought. How could we be greedy?

Kids from "the ghetto" have very few opportunities to meet, greet, and learn from wealthy white people. That's a shame. The wealthiest white person I met growing up was the landlord of the duplex my family and I moved into after the apartment. He lived in Los Gatos, CA. As a track and field athlete in high school, I raced in many cities around the Bay Area. Los Gatos was one of the ritziest. It turned out our landlord also had competed in track and field, and we were able to have a few conversations about the sport as he checked on his property. It felt weird to me, having a white person at my house. It felt weird talking to one who was not my teacher or coach.

That's how sheltered I was back then. Yet another mistake I made. I could've asked my landlord to introduce me to his teenage grandkids. I could've had rich white friends in Los Gatos to hang out with sometimes. It could've opened up my world to new perspectives, a shift in my thinking. But I let my narrow mindedness make the decision to "keep it real," as we would say back then. "Staying real," meant only associating with people on the inside— poor people and other minorities. I learned later in my life that successful people are not sheltered and they definitely don't allow groupthink to enter their lives. They have powerful connections with people from all walks of life.

As a young man, I was missing valuable exposure to wealth education.

What is wealth education? Wealth education is the knowledge of how money works, and how to put it to work. Wealth education keeps people from falling into money traps.

I can recall seeing these infomercials on television during the '80s as I flipped through channels. These old white guys were talking to an audience or the camera, sharing "secrets" on how to get rich. Most of them were real estate investors with a "proven system" of wealth creation and building. They had hot girls at their sides, showed off their yacht, cars, and mansion. Because of all of the poverty around me, what I saw in these infomercials and movies made me believe wealthy white guys were just like Scrooge McDuck, greedy. They were bad for America and struggling poor people who never had enough.

The truth is, wealthy white people are some of the best citizens in this country. They donate to charities, start non-profit agencies to support a worthy cause, and establish foundations that help women and children all over the world. Your school may even be sponsored or funded by a wealthy white person. For example, many schools in Los Angeles have the Bill and Melinda Gates foundation to thank for technology, training, innovation, and other types of grants. Warren Buffett, one of the wealthiest persons on the planet has given his billions to Bill and Melinda Gates, to support their educational outreach.

I need you to give yourself permission to learn from wealthy white people. You need to forget how you may feel about them if it's negative, and give wealthy whites the benefit of the doubt. You need to realize their contributions to society benefit many people and that they have answers you must have questions for. For example:

How can I become wealthy like you?
How can I become as successful as you did?
How do you continue to stay on top and grow your wealth?
How would you start today?

These are a few questions you should have ready at all times for wealthy people of any ethnicity. Wealthy white people are no different. They've learned how to make insane sums of money. They've learned how to have money work for them. This is a skill you desperately need to have for yourself if you're to escape the cycle of poverty.

What's the cycle of poverty? The cycle of poverty is when poor families get trapped being poor so that it is passed down from one generation to the next without end.

If you don't know any wealthy white people, your next best course of action is to discover what they've already taught the world. I'm going to introduce you to some names that have penned valuable lessons on success. Find books written by Napoleon Hill, Stephen Covey, Brian Tracy, John C. Maxwell, Anthony "Tony" Robbins, and Jack Canfield, to name just a few. You can read what they have to share at your local library or bookstore. I've read their books and it's made a huge difference in my life.

Don't let the previous suggestion go in one ear and out the other. I'm aware that some of you would rather be slaves to your own ideas of how the world works. Much like I did, you believe you have it all figured out and you prefer listening to the noise being made by the ignorant.

Ignore the noise from the ignorant and for the ignorant

The world is a noisy place full of distraction, especially in America. Successful people learn to turn the noise down, or mute it. Successful people can't afford to listen to any of the noise meant for the ignorant, made possible by ignorance. Turn on any television, go on any news media online, touch open your social media apps, listen to your favorite hip-hop station, and you will see this being fed to you: Racism, violence, stupidity, fear, power, and happy or sad endings. Most of you can't get enough of this junk.

You've been programmed all of your life to tune into ignorance. Don't believe me? Think of the last bit of gossip or drama you heard about at school. Was it about someone being racist? Was it about a fight? Did someone do something stupid? Did it involve someone being scared? Did a group exert its power over someone? Was someone happy or sad with an outcome?

Your brain is a powerful organ. To make living easier, the brain makes people form habits that become automatic and difficult to break. For instance, everyone struggles to ride a bike for the first time. But if you keep trying to learn and don't give up, eventually your mind is able to tell your body what to do so you don't fall again. After you've learned to ride a bike, you never forget. What you see and hear on television and social media has the same effect on your mind as learning to ride a bike.

The noise you tune into builds bad habits. For example, if a bully starts to harass another person on your social network of choice, you tune in and become a spectator. You might even feel an adrenaline rush from the interactions the bully and victim are having. If you're not going to step in and help the victim, the least you can do is leave the platform. You're actually helping the bully out by providing an audience. But some of you can't help going back to the thread, and being part of the online drama even as a spectator. It's a bad habit you need to break if success is your desire.

Racism is probably one of the most addictive types of distractions that exist in the U.S. People can't get enough of it. Whether they see acts of racism on video, or happening before their very eyes, racism is like a drug your brain is dependent on. In schools, racism can completely destroy a learning environment. Seeing fights between Latinos and Blacks, or whites wearing Confederate flag t-shirts, is a whole lot more exciting than learning how to use the Pythagorean Theorem. Admit it. School is more interesting to you when there is controversy. However, if you can't turn off the switch in your ear that is highly sensitive to the noise I've described, what does that make you?

I have something I do every time I'm confronted with noise in my life. In my mind I scream as loud as I can the word, "noise!" This has the effect of scaring me away from paying attention. If you really want to be successful one day, I want you to add something else to your current list of fears— killing time. It's the fear of killing valuable time, of being ignorant, that stops me from giving more of my life away. I know I won't live forever so I must use and not abuse every minute of my life. In other words, my attention has to be earned and so should yours. Try the following exercise to break the habit you have of letting noise pollute your mind.

Put "Noise" on Alert:

You have to put racism, violence, stupidity, and other ignorance on alert. I'm going to give you some scenarios. As soon as you finish reading each one, you have to immediately yell, "Noise!" I want to be able to hear you across this page. Ready?

1. A friend comes over and tells you someone is talking bad about you.

2. You get a Snapchat message, open it and it's a picture of a girl making an embarrassing face. Your friend captions it, "Ugly ..."

3. As you're walking to class two boys start yelling profanities at each other. They get in each other's face. A crowd begins to form.

4. You're on Facebook and you see a post about a politician or politics with 28 comments. You can tell the conversation has gotten heated.

5. Your friend tells you that another friend of yours is "talking" to your ex-boyfriend.

As a young person, you have the hardest time hitting the power-off button on the negativity around you. It's because your emotions constantly seek validation in the emotions of others. Emotions are a type of energy that is difficult to control at your age. Putting "noise" on alert helps you become aware of your emotions becoming activated and being hijacked. By yelling the word, "noise," in your mind, you take back control of your emotions and short circuit the stimulation that reinforces the bad habit. In effect, you start to dismiss interruptions and keep your focus.

Three types of people

There are three types of people:

1) The ignorant
2) Those that passively absorb knowledge
3) Those that actively seek knowledge

When I was in middle school, I was a member of the ignorant club. I loved the noise more than I loved myself. I focused on the lives of the popular kids and whatever drama unfolded at school. To fit in, I purposely acted up in class, leading to multiple referrals to the office.

I sincerely regret how I acted with one teacher in particular: Ms. Paine. Ms. Paine was a brand new teacher, fresh out of college. She was white like many of my other teachers at the time so it wasn't her ethnicity that made her my target. It was her youth and inability to be legit. The poor woman had no idea how to work with a class full of minorities. Thrown checkers, kids leaping outside off the bungalow window, insults, and absolutely zero learning took place on a daily basis in Ms. Paine's class. Regrettably, we made Ms. Paine cry several times. We were awfully ignorant.

There's plenty of ignorance to go around. Ignorance doesn't discriminate. It can show itself in any person at any time. However, people who continue to passively absorb knowledge are less susceptible to the noise of the ignorant, and it keeps them from making their own ignorant noise sometimes. Who are people who absorb knowledge passively? Students!

If it weren't for schools or institutions of higher learning, most people wouldn't be consumers of knowledge. As a young person, you're forced to go to school to get an education. But what if you weren't? What would your day to day be like without school? You already have a good idea. Just think of what you do during your summer or winter vacations. Let me guess, you play video games, hang out with friends, be on your phone, maybe play a sport or do a physical activity, eat, and sleep. You're used to others providing knowledge; you're not used to getting it for yourself. I can assure you that you'll never have enough to eat and you'll starve if your teachers are the only ones serving you a knowledge plate. Get up off that chair and fix your own!

Successful people separate themselves from the ignorant and passive sponges of knowledge. Successful people avoid anything to do with ignorant people because they have nothing to offer. Successful people live to actively seek new knowledge, the type that can modify their perceptions of what they already know. This excellent habit allows successful people to continuously make breakthroughs in their lives. Indeed, actively seeking knowledge saved and continuous to shape my life every day.

Sometime after my first semester of high school, one that was no different than my three years of middle school, I started to hang out with more scholarly students. I found out right away that I was incredibly behind. I could tell I wasn't the smartest of the bunch. The one thing I had going for me was a lot of freedom to come and go at home. I knew how to get around the city of San Jose on the bus. Instead of using my bus pass on the weekends to go visit friends, I rode the bus to the downtown library. I would arrive before opening hours, and I would leave in the evening. A packed lunch was all I needed. This was before the Internet and personal computers.

Going to the library was a great excuse for me to be out of the house. I would load my backpack with food, a textbook, and a notebook, and tell my mother where I was going. That was enough to keep my father at bay. When he got home after his Sunday side gigs, he wouldn't be able to find me. He had to hold every ill word he had saved for me about my lack of doing chores. He valued education, and he was willing to forego giving me a tongue lashing if I was studying.

I enjoyed my time at the downtown library. It had three floors I could explore and books on every topic. My favorite place to sit at was the Martin Luther King Jr. area. The library was named after the civil rights leader. It was there that I read such works as, The Autobiography of Malcolm X by Alex Haley, Letters from a Birmingham Jail by M.L.K, Jr., Mohandas K. Ghandi's autobiography: The Story of My Experiments with Truth, and selected speeches of Cesar Chavez.

To this day I prefer to seek knowledge from books than from online resources. I love how a book feels in my hands. A great habit that began for me in high school endures to this day. Seeking knowledge actively explains a lot of my personal success. If I were to do my youth all over again, I would've started actively seeking knowledge sooner. I would also vary what I was reading. I spent too much time reading political science. In a later chapter, I will reveal to you what type of knowledge is best to look for and learn from today.

Chapter 1 Main Points:

1. Don't fall for groupthink, as it will stifle your personal growth.
2. Obsessing about racism consumes too much time and energy, not to mention it makes it easier for you to use blame.

3. Give yourself the okay to learn the success secrets of wealthy whites. They are no more or less greedy than you are.
4. You must work at shutting out all the noise in your life. Tuning in to noise is a bad habit.
5. You'll care less about noise by becoming an active knowledge seeker.

Chapter 2
Reframing Your Problems

What if I told you that your problems were your biggest gifts in life? You'd probably think I was joking. Think about it like this, your problems provide you with opportunities to become resourceful and creative. One of the biggest problems I had as an adolescent was not having parents with money. It meant I had to wear clothes and shoes from discount stores. I felt so embarrassed. I also dreaded the start of each school year because other kids would show up wearing Nike shoes and the clothing of expensive name brands like Guess and Starter.

During the summer prior to the start of seventh grade, I decided to buy myself one new outfit. I was going to look good at the start of the year for once. I thought of several ways I could earn money and came up with three possibilities.

We didn't own a lawnmower so I couldn't mow lawns. But my dad did own a nice metal rake. I went around the neighborhood asking the few homeowners with front yard trees if I could rake the leaves off their driveways and lawns for five dollars. Some said, "Yes," and some said "No." My dad preferred to drink his beer out of aluminum cans. I started crushing them and placing them in a large garbage bag until I had enough to take to the recycling center. I'd get back anywhere from $8 to $15 each visit. The last way I came up with making money that summer was pure genius.

The duplex I lived in was two streets away from the housing complex San Jose State University reserved for its scholarship athletes. Many of the residents were members of the football team. I recruited two of my friends and we went around knocking on doors asking these huge athletes if they'd hire us to clean their kitchens. They were so messy they'd invite us in even before I finished our service pitch. We charged ten dollars. I kept five and gave my friends $2.50 each since the business was my idea.

By finally seeing my parent's lack of money as an opportunity, I was able to purchase the clothes and footwear I wanted each school year after sixth grade. I made even more money in 8th grade and was able to replace my entire wardrobe. I joined a crew of teenagers driven around in a van throughout the Bay Area, selling subscriptions door to door to the San Jose Mercury News. I made anywhere from $150 to $260 a month. I'd give some of my money to my mother so she could buy more groceries. For once in my life, I witnessed my father proud of me.

Successful people reframe their problems as opportunities. They ask themselves questions that get their minds working on solutions. The solutions may not be obvious or fast to come to mind. Nonetheless, they keep thinking. When I didn't have nice clothes to wear in middle school, I didn't allow the fact that I couldn't afford them stop me. I asked myself this question: How can I afford them? As you read above, that led to three great solutions. If approached with the correct mindset, your problems can give you an endless infusion of creativity and determination. If you don't let your problems defeat you, they can actually make your mind stronger.

Don't let your problems define you

I let myself be labeled by my problems too much as a kid. Living as an immigrant, I constantly felt like I didn't belong. English was my second language, and while in elementary, I wasn't very good at speaking it. Kids made fun of me for pronouncing words incorrectly. I got fed up with it. I decided to be the best English as a Second Language (E.S.L) student in my class. I was the first one to finish memorizing how to spell words and take the one-on-one spelling test with my teacher. I volunteered to do errands for teachers, putting myself in a situation where I'd have to speak English. I even practiced speaking English at home.

One day my 4th grade teacher announced that there were open positions for student body president, vice president, and treasurer. I had two years of learning English under my belt and I was no expert. I raised my hand anyway and volunteered to run for treasurer. I had to write a speech and deliver it in the cafeteria in front of the entire 4th grade class! It was very nerve-racking, but I did it anyway and won. You may be thinking right now, great little story there, Homie G, it really made me feel fuzzy and warm on the inside. It's not what I have just shared with you that matters most. It's what I haven't shared with you yet that you need to stick around for.

You see, during elementary, when I was most innocent and vulnerable, my father was going through some difficult times. Already a drinker, he took to drinking even more and he had a bad temper. The combination of bad temperament and alcohol consumption don't go well together. At the time, I happened to be my father's translator everywhere he went. The first words out of his mouth every time I messed up translating for him, once we were alone in the car, were, "What good is all that school if you can't translate for me? You're a good for nothing!" It crushed my spirits and forced me to often question my self-worth.

My father had a way of getting his point across when words weren't enough. He'd grab his belt and strike me with fury. Most kids get spanked occasionally. During elementary, I was hit violently once, sometimes twice a month. The corporal punishment lasted until around the time I was twelve. What kept me going? What helped me face my problems and persevere?

Like I mentioned before, your brain is a very powerful organ. One day after a beating, when I was left crying alone as usual, I decided I'd stop trying to make sense of it all. It was pointless. Instead, I started to visualize myself as an older and stronger me. I was taller, muscular like a bodybuilder, and even knew how to fight. In my mind, I'd see the day when my father would no longer have dominion over my body. Visualization was a powerful tool I had at my disposal, and I even used it while receiving beatings to feel numb inside. No adult or situation could take that away from me.

I turned to visualization whenever I felt my problems become too much a part of my identity, a part of who I was. Visualization also helped me maintain a positive outlook about my future. So long as you believe the future is in your hands, yours to choose what to do with, the images you create will be powerful incentives to keep on fighting. Try the following out.

Visualization Exercise:

In a few seconds, I want you to close your eyes and think about the future. Put yourself somewhere, anywhere except the place where all of your problems live. Ready? The year is 2026. What are you up to? What have you accomplished? Where are you living? Now close your eyes and visualize for 30 seconds.

On a piece of paper, write down everything you saw in your vision.

You will see that as you do this exercise over and over, your images will become more colorful. You will also discover that you have much more to write about. However, you can't do this once and be done. Like any skill, it takes lots of practice to get great at it. Successful people always have a clear vision of their immediate and long-term future selves. Even though I'm 40 years old, and I've accomplished many things, I still do this exercise once a week. My life isn't over!

I recommend you visualize the positive future ahead of you at least twice a week, until you are confident what you envision will one day happen, and your body starts responding in turn. Even to this day I feel discomfort right after I visualize. My anxiety becomes my best friend because it gets me to question my current level of activity. Am I doing enough to realize the future I desire? What can I do more of? Can what I'm currently doing be acting as a roadblock in any way? These are questions that follow my visualization sessions. I answer them right below my written vision of the future me.

With a visualizing mind, your body will have no choice but to commit to whatever constructive action is placed in front of it. Otherwise there's really no point to visualizing. What's even better, you will see that when there's nothing you have assigned, you will look for enrichment activities on your own. Taking action to live out your visions is 90% of the success equation. The other 10% belongs to having written goals. There will be more on both of these topics in the ensuing chapters.

You can't choose your problems; your problems choose you

Every person has problems, but not everyone deals with them in the same way. How you deal with your problems makes all the difference in the world. No one chooses his or her problems. They arise out of circumstance. Since you can't choose your problems, the only thing you can do is not let them choose you. When you allow problems to dominate your thinking and behavior, you become the chosen one. You become a sufferer, victim, and troubled soul. You start feeling sorry for yourself and pity everything about you.

I've worked with thousands of students and every last one of them had "problems." Parent problems, girlfriend or boyfriend problems, money problems, friend problems, etc., the list goes on and on. Most of you will deal with these problems with alcohol and/or marijuana. Some of you will even try hurting yourself. How do I know this? This is all many of you know. It was all I knew.

Although I shunned drugs and alcohol during high school, I let loose in college, especially during my first and second year. I smoked marijuana multiple times, and consumed a lot of alcohol from Friday to Sunday. I used this lame excuse: UC Santa Barbara is a party school, so why not party? And lots of partying I did. In truth though, I was trying to mask my emotional pain. I was trying to cope with pressure and stress the only way I knew how. I'd learned how to cope from my father, Mexican movies, music, and friends. These were all poor examples to follow that offered little in the form of positive coping strategies. So I drank, cried in private, and made many poor decisions.

The people in your lives while you are young, parents, teachers, uncles, aunts, older siblings, and so on, spend most of their time telling you not to do drugs. They tell you drugs are "bad," and "drugs can kill." It's true, but not what you want to hear. So you know, they're doing this to keep you safe and to protect your life's potential. Unfortunately, most adults fall short of making a deep and lasting impact on you.

Parents are afraid to admit to their children that *they* have problems. They don't want to seem weak. They want to portray to you all of the courage and strength they can muster so that you have nothing to be afraid of. That's very honorable of them. However, it's not always the right move.

One of my favorite movies is, The Pursuit of Happyness, starring Will Smith. It's the story of Chris Gardner, one of my video mentors. Mr. Gardner was under extreme duress, homeless while caring for his son. He lived with his son for some time at a Bay Area Rapid Transport (BART) station in the Bay Area. What I most appreciated while watching the film was how the character of Mr. Gardner (Smith) communicated with his son. He was frank, vulnerable at times, and didn't try to hide the obvious from his son. He was very human.

All of you are very perceptive. You can tell when your parents are struggling, despite their valiant efforts to hide things from you. I know deep down from my experience that it would matter more to you if your parents admitted their faults, mistakes, and struggles with you more often. If they, for example, could tell you that doing drugs is the way people try to relieve their emotional or physical pain, wouldn't that make more sense than, "Don't do drugs because drugs are bad"? If they told you that doing drugs is what people who can't live in their world do to escape their reality, would that make you think twice about doing drugs? You see drugs aren't about fun and games. Drugs are about life and death.

As an assistant principal, I witnessed many kids poisoning themselves with drugs. Some of them sickened themselves so much they had to be rushed to the hospital to have their stomachs pumped. The sad thing was that these teens didn't just hurt themselves; they also scared and hurt their parents (and younger siblings) very badly. I also spent many hours asking students who were under the influence, and sober enough to talk, this question: So what hurts? The immediate response I got, almost 100% of the time was, "Nothing." Eventually I'd break down their walls, get to the root of the problem, and offer counseling, Homie G style.

Doing drugs won't help your problems go away. In fact, self-medicating only leads to more problems. Addiction, which is both a chemical and physical reliance on a drug of choice, is one major problem drug abuse can lead to. There are ways to handle your problems that don't involve the use of drugs. You may have had someone, a counselor or therapist, for example, share some positive ways to get a "natural high." These include doing sports, dancing, meditation, and Yoga.

In his best-selling book, Be Obsessed or Be Average, multi-millionaire sales coach, investor, and author, Grant Cardone, provides a unique method on how people can crush their problems. Mr. Cardone (another one of my video mentors) spent many years of his early life as a drug addict until hitting, "rock-bottom." Thankfully, he discovered after this awful period of his life that he was happiest when he was obsessed with being the best at his craft: selling. He switched a negative obsession, doing drugs, with a positive one, creating a system he could sell to businesses to improve their sales. Mr. Cardone recommends everyone obsess about something positive or risk allowing negativity to enter their life.

During high school, I had several personal problem deflectors operating at all times. I participated in two running sports and obsessed about both of them. In addition to constantly training after school, I'd read the magazines my coach would have in his office, and watch videos of elite athletes competing at meets. I idolized track stars like Carl Lewis, Gail Devers, and Arturo Barrios. I'd also go to the mall and window shop at the most expensive retail stores, especially those with running gear. I played pick-up basketball for hours at the closest park, went to comic book stores, and killed hours at the arcade. With so many mental distractions, I never had time to let my problems fester. Below you will find other ways you can stop problems from bothering you.

Ways You Can Keep Your Problems from Choosing You:

1. Stay busy. Downtime gives your brain time to think nonsense.
2. Repeat as often as possible, especially when your thoughts become negative: "Positive Mental Attitude!"
3. Write down each of your problems in one column. Call it, "My problems." On the other column, call it, "My Opportunities," write down every opportunity your problem offers you. Be creative.
4. Meditate. Meditation is actually making its way into more public schools as an alternative to discipline.
5. Remove yourself from, change, or accept your situation. Holding onto bitterness is letting your problems own you.
6. Read inspiring real life stories books.
7. Volunteer at a soup kitchen. Helping others less fortunate than you connects your mind with your heart, something we all don't do enough of.
8. Pray for yourself. Pray for others.
9. Keep a journal of your problems. Write how they make you feel and how you managed your feelings on a given day. Turn the journal into a self-help book for teens so your positive message can reach others like you.
10. Be grateful for your problems. This takes away all of their negative energy.

Chapter 2 Main Points:

1. Think of your problems as opportunities to test your abilities, creativity, and resourcefulness.

2. You can step away from your problems with visualization.
3. Drugs create more problems and solve nothing.
4. Replace problems with a positive obsession or with activity.

Chapter 3
Check Your Expectations & Take Profitable Action

You are not what you expect, and you never will be. You are what you *do*. Or conversely, you aren't what you fail to do. Go back and re-read the last few sentences if they confused you. If you missed it, they had to do with "doing," because no person on earth has ever reached their full potential with mere expectations. It's true what they say, "It takes blood, sweat, and tears," to be the greatest.

If the world paid people for what they know, there'd be no money left for anything else. We have millions of smart people on Earth. Some of them are even considered geniuses. Fortunately for the economies of every country, people get paid for what they do, not what they know. This is why anyone can become successful. Although it doesn't hurt to have, success doesn't require book smarts; it requires action.

After junior college, far too late in my life, I started to notice something odd. There were a lot of let's just say, not so smart, people telling others and me what to do. If I wanted to get paid, I needed to do as they instructed. These people were bosses or owners. Now I don't want to give you the idea that all bosses are dumb. I've worked for a few textbook smart employers. I want to make sure you understand that success is not limited by what you've failed to learn from textbooks.

Success is actually more closely related to how often you can manage to apply what you learned in books or from other people. Apply in this case means putting to good use. It's a skill to read something informational and figure out how to apply it to your own life. Successful people read with the objective of making their own, owning, as much information as possible. Once information is theirs, they can decide how and when to use it. If you have the fortune of working for a successful business owner, don't do what I did and insult their intelligence. Respect them. They have done with their lives what you will need to do with your own: act, and not just think!

So what's the goal of almost every teacher and adult in your life? That's right…to teach you what they know and how to think. You may pick up some skills at school taking electives, or at home from your industrious parents, but the truth of the matter is, you're not being taught how to take what I call, Profitable Action. Before exploring what Profitable Action is, let's discuss the various types of expectations young people have and how these can set them up for big disappointments or huge triumphs.

Don't expect anything from your parent(s)

There are only three things you should expect from your parents: to be fed, clothed, and housed. Anything else your parents provide you with, for example, love, attention, and care, are assets.

What are assets? Assets are useful and valuable things. People can also be considered assets. For example, "Maria is an asset to the company."

I expected too much from my parents. I expected them to buy me toys, nice clothes, and Air Jordan shoes. I also expected they give me money, words of encouragement, and a bedroom to sleep in. What I actually got was knockoffs from the flea market, shoes from Payless, enough change for the transit bus, an absence of praise, a pillow, blanket, and a couch.

Kids today like you expect like kids of my generation did. You expect your parents to buy you expensive smart phones with unlimited data plans, video game consoles, trendy clothes, and other material items. Even when your parents have little money to carve out an existence for you and the rest of your family, you still manage to squeeze them for things they can't really afford. The fact is many of you are spoiled. Many of you don't deserve what you annoyed your parents into finally getting you. You don't work hard enough, yet you demand what other spoiled and lazy kids have. Harsh? Harsh is being homeless or not being able to feed your future family. So keep reading.

Another one of my all-time favorite movies is, The Blind Side, the story of NFL offensive lineman, Michael Oher. Michael is homeless, feeding himself from the leftover food he picks up off the bleachers after games at his school. Highlighted in the movie are Michael's protective instincts. These, and his size, are the key to his *expected* success on the field. At practice, reality quickly sets in for the football coach, and Michael's latest caretaker, Leigh Anne

Tuohy. Michael doesn't know how to intensify his actions. He lets smaller players on the team get around him without a fight. It's a great metaphor for life. When life pushes people, some let it happen while others push back. What do you do?

It took a mind hack to get Michael to release his inner beast.

What's a mind hack? A mind hack is similar to hacking or breaking through the security of a computer to access it, except in this case the computer is your brain. You or someone else can hack your mind and place suggestions in your head that get you to think or even do things differently. It is not hypnosis.

Leigh Anne disrupted practice, pulled Michael aside, and forced him to focus differently. At the time, Michael's focus was centered on football being a game of no consequence. Leigh Anne raised the stakes. She told Michael to think of his new adoptive family, the people he cares enough about to protect, as players on the offense. The players on the defense were there to hurt his family, and he needed to stop them.

Leigh Anne's mind trick involved having Michael associate a seemingly difficult physical task with one that is instinctual. If you've ever seen people jump to action, like a mother grabbing an infant before falling from a dangerous height, you know there are things our bodies will do without thinking. Leigh Anne could've just said: "Michael, it's in your nature to protect this quarterback and this tailback." That wouldn't have worked. She knew she had to make Michael create a powerful association between his reluctance to go "all out" and his true potential. You can do this too! Let me show you how below.

Association Exercise:

Think of something that could change your life, but that you've been reluctant to get started. This could be a small business, school club, blog, project to help the environment, your first eBook, an exercise program, or saving for a future expense. Now imagine something that would be painful to lose. This could be a family heirloom, the only picture of a loved one, a pet, a valuable collectible, or the respect of someone you care about. Let's call these, "association tokens."

Now imagine the actual loss of your association token. You worked hard all of your life to care for, nurture, or conserve your association token and now it's gone forever. Are you feeling sad and upset? Let the emotion build up inside of you until you can no longer tolerate it. Remember this feeling every time an adult tells you you're underachieving or being lazy. Pretend you will lose something priceless to you if you don't release *your* inner beast and get to it. Repeat this exercise daily to remain beastly.

Your parents are individuals, first, parents, second

Not highlighted in The Blind Side is an extremely important life lesson every adolescent and teen should learn: Expectations impact your life tremendously. Back to the expectations many young people have of their parents. Many adolescents believe the number one job of their guardian is to be a parent. Wrong! The number one job of a guardian is to be who they are. They can be more, but sometimes choose not to.

The harshest words I've ever had to tell kids in private are: "Your father may never be the man you want him to be." Or worse yet: "Don't expect your mother to ever change for you." This made many of them cry, but crying was actually progress. Remember my situation? I had a father who drank himself into evil incarnate on most evenings. I expected him to be a good dad. "Why can't he just stop drinking for me?" I'd often say to myself. I took it very personal. Well, it never happened while I lived in his house. There is a "happy ending" in my case. My father would eventually stop drinking. According to his doctor, he was dangerously close to having cirrhosis of the liver. He's been sober for almost two decades now. Our relationship has improved greatly and I forgave him many years ago.

Unfortunately, there may be no turnaround or "happy ending" for you. I'm not telling you this to upset you. I'm telling you this so you don't take what your parents do so personal. So you can begin to live your life for you, and not for anyone else or in spite of anyone else. So you can have self-reliance.

What is self-reliance? Self-reliance is relying on your own efforts, abilities, and resources. It's the opposite of dependence.

Michael Oher was self-reliant. In the movie, Michael never complained about his mother. She was a drug addict, brought strange men over the house, and parented horribly. Still, Michael had come to terms with who his mother was and moved on. He kept taking steps, literally walking down streets at night, until Mrs. Tuohy spotted him one evening.

Similarly, Michael didn't expect anything from the Tuohy's. He didn't expect to be taken on a shopping spree for clothes, to be given a bedroom of his own (with a bed!), to be given the keys to a new truck, or to be finally living in the home of a family worthy of him. Yet all this happened. I'm convinced it's because he expected only of himself and didn't allow the adults in his life to disappoint him into giving up.

Don't expect your parents to love you, give you the attention you deserve, and take care of you. If these things are happening now, great! You have a wonderful thing going for you so cherish it. Adults with children simply can't be parents first. They were born individuals and they will die individuals. This means they have a biological desire to meet their own needs first. Once their kids stop being children, adults resume behaving more and more like individuals. Yes, this means they get more selfish. Understand that this is natural. As you get older, you are doing exactly the same, defining your individualism.

Counselors and therapist will ask you how you feel about things. "And how does that make you feel?" they may have asked you in private. Aren't they annoying sometimes? You end up disliking therapy sessions because you're never told what you already know deep down: the therapist can't change your parents, and neither can you. That's what you want, right? Someone to change your parents. But it will never happen like this. Your guardians are like all people, locked inside by a change gate that they alone can (and many times refuse to) open. There is no point to laying blame on your guardians if you think your life is "messed up." They are who they are. You are who you are. Therefore, you're responsible for your own happiness. Not anyone else. And the truth shall set you free.

If only someone had broken it down for me like this when I was an adolescent. Maybe I would have risen from the floor sooner. I realize now that I expected too many things to come my way from adults, and not enough of myself. The sooner you wean yourself off your parents' assistance, the faster you'll become self-reliant.

What is Profitable Action?

Profitable Action is the beneficial and accumulating action one takes to accomplish a goal. I like to describe any other type of action as, "Dead Chicken Action." There is a popular saying: "Running around like a headless chicken." It's a scientific fact that if not decapitated correctly by a butcher a dead chicken can run around aimlessly until its muscles stop twitching. Symbolically, this is what the majority of all people are doing, including you. Dead Chicken Action is aimless, clumsy, fatiguing, and deadly to success.

On his blog, Brian Tracy, the premiere authority on the topic of personal success, writes that less than 3% of all Americans have written goals and only 1% review and rewrite their goals daily. So what? Mr. Tracy, as well as multiple other authorities on success found that there is something in common the wealthiest and most successful people in America have. They write out, review, revise, and take action on their goals. This is why the most important aspect of Profitable Action is that it's goal oriented.

Profitable Action has three components. One, it's beneficial to you. This can take many forms. For

example, exercising benefits your health. Saving your allowance helps you make a later purchase. Studying for tests benefits your grades and can even improve your chances of getting into a top university.
Shooting free throws daily makes it more likely you'll make them in a game. What you take part in must be useful. If it isn't, consider yourself headless poultry.

      Two, Profitable Action is accumulating. This means that the action you take must build on itself like money earning interest in an account. Case in point, if one of your goals is to run a half-marathon, you train daily. You need to vary the volume and intensity of your workouts. You wouldn't just go on a 4-mile run one time and show up on race day. If another one of your goals is to learn how to code before graduating from high school, then you'd take beginning, intermediate, and advanced courses at school, online, or at training academies. Imagine packing snow from a small ball into the base of a snowman. That's accumulating action.

      Finally, Profitable Action is goal driven. Here is where we separate the super successful from the average. Super successful people undertake activities that serve a greater purpose, to meet a goal. Average people participate in activities that have disconnected purposes or no purposes at all. That's why average people don't get anywhere. If ever there was an expression to describe not taking Profitable Action, it is: "You're all over the place!"

      Below is an exercise that will make writing goals and taking Profitable Action fun for you.

Two Jars, One Bright Future, Exercise:

      Whenever you write out a goal, pay yourself $1. Simply take a piece of white paper, size doesn't matter, and write "$1" on it. Drop this slip of paper into an empty and clean spaghetti sauce jar. Label the jar, "My future-Goals," with a Sharpie. There is no limit to how often you can make a deposit. If you write out five goals, place 5, $1 deposit slips into the jar.

Get another jar and label it, "My future-Action." In this jar, you will deposit $100 dollar slips every time you take decisive action on a goal. You may be wondering why taking action earns you $100 of funny-money while writing a goal only makes you $1. Taking action on a goal is 100 times more difficult to do! You have to get past your fears and doubts, and put your body in motion. People fear failure. They let doubt overtake their thought process so much they won't even try. Have you ever told yourself: "That won't work," or "I'm not good enough," or my personal favorite, "I don't have time"? These are the excuses both lazy and/or fearful people give to keep from challenging themselves.

This exercise is true to life. Those that take goal directed action win at life. Those that don't will struggle at life constantly. Your jars will be visual reminders of how hard you're working on your future. The jars help you keep score. You'll see that after a few deposits, you'll start really getting into it. You'll get the urge to keep doing it. Using this strategy is not silly or stupid. Silly or stupid is expecting money, fame, health, love, intelligence, success, to come knocking on your door.

Chapter 3 Main Points

1.   You'll get paid for what you *do*, not what you know.

2. Expecting your parents to provide for your emotional and physical needs can lead to disappointment.
3. Becoming self-reliant keeps you from blaming others and helps you always move forward.
4. Taking Profitable Action is the only way you'll avoid being a Dead (headless) Chicken.

Chapter 4
Write Goals Down & Expect Positive Outcomes

Because of my wasteful and destructive behavior in middle school, counselors at Yerba Buena High School in San Jose placed me in remedial math. The class was called, Math-A. Before I could get into Algebra 1, I had to pass this course *and* Math-B. According to my counselors, I was behind two levels. My Math-A teacher gave us worksheets and blocks to play with all period. I was so bored. The only time I was ever engaged was when my teacher would bring in his stock portfolio. He'd show us pieces of papers called, "stocks," and tell us they were worth lots of money. He'd tell us the stocks represented ownership in various companies. "You own McDonald's?" I asked him once. "No," he said. "As a shareholder, I'm part owner of McDonald's, along with thousands of people."

Even though I enjoyed learning about stocks from my 9th grade Math-A teacher, I didn't want to sit in his class another year in Math-B. In my gut I felt I could handle Algebra 1. But I was stuck. The counselors had a rule about not placing students into other classes once the semester was well underway. They didn't want to "inconvenience" the teachers and used the excuse that I'd be too far behind to catch up with everyone else in the Algebra 1 class.

If I had written out a goal after 8th grade graduation that included starting Algebra 1 as a high school freshman, maybe I would've advocated for myself at freshman registration. I could've easily walked up to the counselors' table and said, "I don't want this Math-A class, I want to take Algebra 1." The counselors may have still said I didn't meet the requirements to get into Algebra 1, but to have met my goal I would've taken Profitable Action until the two-week window to change classes ended, and I got what I wanted. Scheduling an appointment with the Principal to talk to him about my request is an example of the Profitable Action I could've taken after being told, "No," by the counselors.

I didn't do any of those things though. Instead I took Dead Chicken Action, and let life simply decapitate me. After I'd had enough of beating myself up for my inaction, I thought hard about what to do about my problem. I made a goal for myself. I decided I would be in Geometry by the start of my sophomore year. At the time, I had no idea how I would do this.

On his blog, Jack Canfield, a success guru and co-founder of the Chicken Soup for the Soul series, presents a powerful success formula: E + R = O. "E" stands for Events. "R" stands for Response. And, "O," stands for "Outcome." The gist of this formula is basically this: the way you respond to the events of your life determines your outcome. I got a bad schedule handed to me as an incoming freshman (event). My response was doing nothing about it. So my outcome didn't change. To get out of Math-A and into Geometry by grade 10, I had to drastically change my response. What did I do? I earned an "A" in Math-A for both semesters. I enrolled in Algebra 1 for summer school, skipping Math-B altogether, and earned two "B's". I had done it. The counselors had no choice but to enroll me in Geometry at the start of my 10th grade year.

Goals give you clear direction and control of your future

Because I had no written goals for high school after 8th grade, I didn't have clear direction and control of my future. I'm quite confident that many of you have left your future up to chance, much like I had in my teenage years. Many of you have already been non-responsive to the events in your life and have suffered outcomes you didn't want. Your future will be one enormous question mark if you don't spell out what you want for yourself. You need to take back your future. Doing so begins with keeping a journal of big, medium, and small "S.M.A.R.T" goals. First, you'll need to learn what S.M.A.R.T goals are.

S.M.A.R.T Goal Exercise:

A S.M.A.R.T goal is *S*pecific, *M*easurable, *A*chievable, *R*esults-Oriented, and *T*ime-Bound. You may have been taught this in school. I've taught hundreds of students in my career to write SMART goals. I tell them, however, that I've never liked the "A" in SMART. Too many times my students mistake the "A" in a SMART goal to mean something they can achieve with their *current* skills and knowledge, instead of something that they can achieve with the skills and knowledge they learn along the way. To me, "Achievable" is anything that is humanly possible. Here's a SMART goal my students often write:

Big SMART Goal: By the start of the first semester of my senior year, I will have all of the requirements necessary to get accepted to Cal State San Marcos.

This leads me to ask the student, "So why not Harvard or Stanford?" Their usual response: "I can't get into those schools!"

It's not that you can't get into a top university. You can. You just don't know the type of effort it takes to do so. And you will never know unless you embark on the journey and learn what it takes as you go. You see a SMART goal is only a destination, where you want to end up. It's not the actual journey. Like learning a new dance or figuring out how to get good at a video game, the mistakes you make are signs along the road. Mistakes tell you if you're on course or have veered off course from your destination. This is why it's so important for you to write SMART goals. They represent the first step in your journey toward success, spelling out exactly where you want to be in the future.

My main point is this: If something is humanly possible, then you can achieve it. Despite what you believe you are capable of, you must write goals that are scary for you to imagine, and then take Profitable Action. Successful people set the bar so high for themselves with their goals that they too get scared. But even scarier to them is the thought of being old one day, thinking back, and having regrets because they didn't give their dreams a chance. It frightens me to think of myself as an old man lying on my deathbed wishing I'd had more courage to reach for the stars. This is why my goals are always sky high.

No regrets! Now let's look at what a "Medium" SMART goal looks like.

Medium SMART Goal: By the end of my 10th grade year, I will have the required grade point average and coursework, and at least three extracurricular activities completed to be on track to meet my Big SMART goal.

Notice how the Medium SMART goal feeds into the Big SMART goal. You have to create goals that breakdown a Big SMART goal into chunks. The last piece of this puzzle is writing a Small SMART goal.

Small SMART Goal: By the end of my 9th grade year, I will have researched the California State University requirements, read the entire Cal State San Marcos website, and have visited the campus twice.

The way you decide to break a Big SMART goal down into parts is entirely up to you. Realize that it's necessary to do so because otherwise you can veer off course from your destination and never know it. You also need a source of motivation. Completing Small SMART goals provide you with a sense of accomplishment and strengthen your determination to keep going.

I'm a personal finance blogger at www.commoncoremoney.com. I write articles that help people save and make more money, as well as get out of debt. Many Americans use credit cards irresponsibly, and rack up a bunch of debt on more than one card. A Small SMART goal I often recommend involves people paying off the credit card with the smallest balance first. For example, if they owe $7,000 on one credit card, $3,500 on another, and $1,150 on a third card, I suggest they make the minimum payment on the two credit cards with the higher balances. I also advice they make as big of a payment as they possibly can on the one with the smaller balance. Why? People naturally get excited about completing something difficult. Trying to take on a large debt one payment at a time can be discouraging. People don't like seeing their balance barely budge every month. So they'll feel great about paying off the smaller debt and then want to jump on the next one.

Below is a template you can use to write your SMART goals.

_____ SMART Goal: By _____ (timeframe), I will have or be able to do

_____

_____

_____

_____

____ (results).

SMART Goals need not be about academics. Let me show you examples of non-academic goals.

Fitness: By (insert your date), I will be able to do _____ sit-ups in _____ seconds.

Health: By (insert your date), I will have lost a total of _____ pounds and weigh _____ lbs.

Social: By (insert your date), I will have gone on
_____ date(s) and be courting
_____ (love interest).

Entrepreneurship: By (insert your date), I will have
written a Mission and Vision statement, as well as a
company motto for my new fashion accessories
business,
_____(busine
ss name).

Business: By (insert your date) my fashion
accessories business, (business name), will have
doubled its monthly sales revenue of
_____ (current monthly sales revenue).

Athletics: By (insert your date), I will have shaved off
_____ seconds from my mile time personal record
of _____ (your current mile time).

Family: By (insert your date), I will have thrown out
the garbage at least _____ times before my
father gets home from work so I can avoid getting
yelled at.

Personal Growth: By (insert your date), I will have
read a total of _____ books on the topic of
_____ (an area you can improve
on).

Hobby: By (insert your date), I will be able to land a
_____ stair step jump on my skateboard.

Financial: By (insert your date), I will have made
_____ million dollars.

Let me stress something to you. You're making a huge mistake if you think you can keep your SMART goals in your head. I know many of you don't like to write, but I'm not giving you a hall pass on this one. You must get into the habit of writing your goals on paper. This particular task of committing your goals to paper, if turned into a habit, will one day make you a millionaire. Would you give up millions of dollars because of a few extra minutes a day and a $1 notepad? There is truly something fundamentally powerful that takes place when your eyes see what your hand is writing.

In 2007, Dr. Gail Matthews, a clinical psychologist at Dominican University of California, tracked goal completion in groups of students who wrote down their goals versus those that didn't. Students who wrote their goals down had a 42 percent increase in their goal achievement. So keep your goals on paper and in sight because out of sight is out of mind.

You must expect positive outcomes

What is the difference between an average athlete and a great one? I can think of two things: practice and confidence. A great athlete has had more hours of practice. This advantage on the competition provides her with a source of confidence to tap into. Upon seeing a great athlete in action, the average athlete will quickly discover her skillset is no match and give up trying to win. Her body may still go through the motions, but in her head she knows defeat is coming. In many scholastic sporting events, the game is lost even before the final buzzer is heard.

Great athletes expect to win. They expect to make all of their shots, get a hit each time at the plate, throw strikes, and win the race. They can't imagine any other outcome. If only this phenomenon of athletics and competition translated to the real world. In my career, I've seen far too many outstanding student-athletes tremble before a challenge outside the playing arena. If it doesn't involve doing something physical, their confidence disappears and they cease to expect victories. In the real world, a victory is a "yes." You seek a "yes" from the people you ask for help or from the people who answer doors you knock on. Successful people get what they want by knocking on hundreds of doors knowing the majority of them won't open.

Sometimes positive outcomes in your life happen by accident. A critical moment in my life took place during my first semester of high school. I had earned my fourth referral and was sitting in the vice principal's office. I expected to be suspended from school, a negative but logical outcome of my accumulated mistakes. As my vice principal talked consequences, the school's athletic director walked in his office. "I see you got Carlos here," he said. "You know Carlos?" my vice principal asked, surprised. "Yeah," the athletic director said, casually, "he's going to be joining the track team. He ran a 5:30 mile today."

I had no intention of joining the track team, but hearing the athletic director speak positively about my athletic ability with the vice principal made me feel good. I wanted to feel like that again, however, I had very little choice in the matter. I wasn't suspended that day. The athletic director had saved my behind, and I owed it to him to follow through on my part of the deal. A chance office visit to the vice principal's office by the athletic director changed the course of my life. I stopped being a troublemaker that day and became an athlete.

A positive outcome from a visit to the vice principal's office was something I hadn't expected. Has something like this happened to you? Maybe your parents got off with a warning after being pulled over by a police officer? Maybe your parents came home too tired to deal with you, and instead of letting you have it, they just ordered you to your room? Don't leave the remarkable up to chance. Ask for what you need from the universe, from the gatekeepers that hold the key to your unmet goals, and *expect* the positive to occur. In other words, put out positive vibes in any type of challenging or negative situation.

Let rejections make you, not break you

Beware of rejections. If you treat rejections like venom, they will kill your confidence. If instead you treat rejections like a virus, one day you will become immune to the feelings they bring out in you, and you'll stop fearing getting infected.

Rejections train people to stop thinking positively about their outcomes. I had a standout year in track and field my freshman year. Toward the end of the season, I was running for the varsity team. My sophomore year was even better. I joined the cross-country team, broke several school records, and took first place at league. My name was being mentioned in the daily announcements almost every week. My popularity skyrocketed. This gave me great confidence, but it only showed on the track. I couldn't transfer any of that fearlessness to other areas of my life. One in particular frustrated me the most: my lack of boldness with girls.

I had very little "game" with the ladies. In fact, I had zero "game." I was shy and felt awkward talking to females outside of class. Calling girls at home terrified me. Luckily for me, I wasn't gathering many phone numbers. Why? I wasn't asking! I was too afraid to take a conversation with a crush to the next level. These were my excuses:

1. It's too embarrassing.
2. What if she says, "No"?
3. What if she tells her friends I tried to get her phone number?
4. What if the news of my rejection spreads around school?
5. If I don't get her telephone number my friends will make fun of me.
6. She's way out of my league.

What was I doing here? I was psyching myself out. I'd thrown out the window everything my track coach had taught me about mental preparation before a race. Before every race I'd visualize how I would pace myself and where I'd make my move. I'd see myself crossing the finish line before everyone else. Even when I'd lose a race, I never lost it before stepping onto the track.

When it came to talking with girls, I was visualizing the worst happening. I should've been visualizing the girl I liked enjoying conversations with me. I should've been picturing how smooth I'd be while asking for her number. In fact, I was doing the opposite, seeing everyone else *except* myself winning that glorious teenage boy trophy of the '90s: a torn piece of paper with a girl's telephone number written on it. Are you psyching yourself out too with the opposite sex?

When it came to rejection, back then I was missing a key mental attitude: rejections don't break you, they make you. A successful person has placed himself in a possible rejection scenario thousands of times more than an unsuccessful person. A successful person has been denied what they want hundreds of times. The average person has been rejected only a handful of times in their lives. They get a bad taste in their mouth after the first few rejections, decide they don't like it, and vow never to do that again. They quit asking not realizing that every "no" gets you closer to a "yes." It's a numbers game!

After high school, I dated many beautiful women. From 1994 to 2008, I would go on to ask at least one hundred beautiful women for their telephone number. At least 80 of them said, "No." That means 20 of them said, "Yes"! All that practice expecting positive outcomes, doing the asking, and learning to accept the results made me tough. It prepared me for one of the greatest days of my life: the day I met my wife.

The year was 2008, a Saturday night in September. I was at the La Jolla, CA Marriott hotel dancing Salsa. I spotted a gorgeous African-American lady sitting at a table, staring out at the dance floor. When a song ends at a Salsa club, the men either take a break or look for their next dance partner. If they see a woman they want to dance with, they quickly approach and ask her to dance. Why quickly? To seize the opportunity. The men take action because if they don't, someone else will.

No one asked Jessica (my wife's name) to dance when the next song came on. Maybe the men felt intimidated by her looks? Maybe they didn't see her sitting there looking bored out of her mind? I didn't care. I had to capitalize on this opportunity. I walked across the room and asked her to dance. She said, "Yes." The rest is history. Had I not been practicing how to ask courageously for the things I wanted or needed, learning to be immune to rejection, I may have never met my wife. We wouldn't have the beautiful family we have today:

Figure 1: Picture of the Gomez Family. Featured in Money Magazine on April 2015. Photo by Scott Lacey.

With rejections, nothing changes, and everything changes

Rejections are a penalty free activity. Sure, getting a "No" may bruise your ego for a while, especially at the beginning. But once you realize that nothing changed in your life, those denials will become things of the past quicker each time. When I was in junior college, I needed a part-time job to pay for books, gas and insurance for my car. I really wanted to work at this upscale Mexican restaurant. Even as a busboy I'd be making good money with hourly salary and tips. I did my best at the job interview, but I didn't get the job.

Even though I was naturally upset at being rejected, nothing for me had changed. You see, I'd gone into the job interview without the job, and I came out of the job interview without the job. I was no different! Yet I felt as if I had lost something big. Think back at the times you asked for something and were told, "No." Maybe you asked your parents to buy you expensive shoes, a used car, or the latest smartphone. Or maybe you asked your parents to let you go on a trip with friends, spend the night at a friend's house, or go on a date with a boy. Aside from feeling like a huge injustice was done to you, did anything about you change from being denied? So did doing the asking take anything away from you? These were too easy. You're comfortable asking your guardians for stuff.

Many of you are willing to let comfort hold you back from breakthroughs. Anyone foreign to your circle of comfort, which includes your friends, family, neighborhood, and some teachers, will turn into a scary monster at the thought of you having to ask them for something. I know you've had a handful of "mean" teachers in your life. Did you ever ask any of them for an extension on a project when you had a serious family or personal event keep you from finishing it on time? Many of you work part-time at fast food restaurants or supermarkets. If you feel like you've distinguished yourself, would you step foot in your manager's office today and ask for a raise? Some of you know and admire certain local businessmen and businesswomen. Maybe you pass by their offices or storefronts on the way to school. Have you asked any of them to be your mentor?

I let the fear of rejection stop me from making major advances in my life, especially as a young man. Not having a mentor alone cost me probably millions in income and hours of time. And it was all because I didn't see what I see now: with rejections nothing changes, and everything changes. You must have a "what's there to lose?" attitude. Don't be afraid to "go for it." Just think: If you get a "No," you're in the same spot you were before without whatever it was you were asking for. If, in contrast, you were to get a "Yes," now you've moved up. You've gained something. The risk of asking is zero while the reward in getting could be infinite. So as they say, "ask, ask, and ask."

Chapter 4 Main Points:

1. With written goals, you take back control of your future. Without written goals, you will suffer outcomes you don't want.
2. SMART goals are destinations to your future that come without a map. You make the path up as you go.
3. Rejections don't break you, they make you. Your ego may be slightly bruised from a rejection, but nothing about you has changed. On the other hand if you get an approval, things for you can change dramatically.

Chapter 5
You Have Friends Until You Don't

You think you know someone until you realize you don't really know them at all. I've heard divorced people say that about an ex-spouse too many times. These were once married people who *thought* they had their so called, "life partner," figured out. Some of them spent a few months or years dating, and multiple years living together. These couples then drifted apart slowly. In some cases, the changes were very sudden, causing lots of turmoil in their relationships.

It happened to me. Before I found, Jessica, I had another wife. I met her in college. We dated about a year and half, moved in together, and got married. My marriage with this woman only lasted about three years. The last year of our marriage was awful. Both she and I were miserable. We argued constantly and spent very little time enjoying each other's company. Even with couples' therapy, we couldn't make our marriage work. Fortunately, we were able to get a quick and friendly divorce. We had no children and very few possessions to split up.

Other than the death of a loved one, divorces are one of the most difficult situations adults have to go through. I was sick to my stomach prior to my divorce being final. It was hard to shake off the fact that I had failed big time at something. The people in my life tried to console me. But, by making me have to explain what *I* thought happened, my friends and family only made things worse. You see, ultimately it didn't matter what I thought. My ex-wife had her own version of the story. You have probably experienced a dispute in your life where one person thought you were at fault, and you thought the opposite. If a dispute involves money or property, it can become a legal matter settled in court by a judge. Let me tell you right now that having to go to court over a dispute is stressful; it's best to resolve conflicts with others outside of the legal process when possible.

In the case of my first marriage, the only thing that mattered was that the match I thought would be for life was now over. I needed to shift my attitude back to being positive and learn from my mistakes.

I've shared this about myself to help you make more sense of what I'm going to tell you next.

Your "friends" at school are not your friends

Who are your friends? Are they the kids you hang out with at school? Those are not your friends; they're your acquaintances. After high school, if you're still spending time with the people you hung out with, then you can call these people your friends. In the meanwhile, everyone who's not your boyfriend or girlfriend is simply an acquaintance. And some of them have way too much power over you. You give up too much control of your mind to these groups (groupthink) and individuals, costing you valuable time to work on your personal growth, learning on your own or from other further academically along acquaintances.

As an assistant principal, I had way too many disciplinary cases to deal with involving theft. Thievery, sadly, is an epidemic in public schools. The victim would come to the office and ask for my help in tracking down their expensive cell phone. "What happened?" I'd ask the owner. "I let my friend borrow the phone, and now it's gone." "What do you mean it's gone?" I'd follow up. "Well," they'd say naively, "he says he let someone else hold it, and now no one knows who has it." Some friend, right?

In schools, friends steal from friends all the time. But they do more than that. They also turn on each other. Girls have besties one day, and another day the bestie becomes an enemy. Why? Usually it's because of a boy. Instead of being angry with the boy for "playing" both of them, the besties get furiously upset at each other. If I had a nickel for every time I had to mediate a conflict (because of a boy) between two former "best friends" I'd be a rich man. Young ladies, no boy is worth you losing education time.

It gets worse. There is a code among all of you not to "snitch" on each other. It's a stupid code! Why? Apart from being wrong and unethical to keep information that could help solve crimes or injustices, hardly anyone sticks to it.

When the pressure is on, meaning the person of authority has enough evidence, and when the stakes are high, meaning the person being questioned can be severely punished, everyone eventually folds. You've seen enough mobster and crime movies to know this is true. Your "friends" are the first ones to look out for their own self-interests and "snitch" on you. I have solved and resolved over a thousand cases involving drugs, drug paraphernalia, stolen items, and possession of weapons. Enough to verify the snitch code is a mere illusion many of you believe your so-called friends will live by.

Get over your friends at school. The majority of them are not who you think they are. They have no blood or relationship ties to you. They claim to have "your back" but in a hot administrator's office, they'll stab you in the back. You may be having trouble coming to grips with this right now, but look into your heart and feel the truth. Don't think you ever have to personally look out for anyone else at school. If certain individuals are expecting you to travel everywhere they go, agree with their way of thinking, take action the way they decide, you are not with a friend. You are a follower with a bad leader.

"The Cut List" Exercise: (To be done at home)

Get a piece of line paper and draw a line down the middle. On the left column, write the words, "Don't Make the Cut," at the top. On the top of the right column, write the words, "Make the Cut." Now think of every "friend" you have and spend time with. This could also include your boyfriend or girlfriend.

If any of them influence you into not trying to better yourself, making poor decisions, taking risks with your health or physical well-being, hurting others physically or emotionally, or disregarding the wise counsel of adults, do like Beyoncé and "To the left, to the left." Write their names under the "Don't Make the Cut" heading. If on the other hand, your acquaintances encourage your hard work, your commitment to your responsibilities, your personal growth, and you doing the right thing, write their names under the "Make the Cut" heading.

You may discover that you have a whole lot more names on the left than on the right. If you were honest with yourself, you may have also written the names of some people you consider close to you. I foresee that you will have a difficult time of distancing yourself from the people that "Don't Make the Cut." These people will want to keep pulling you back to them. They will question your loyalty to make you feel guilty. They will generate "noise" at school or on social media to force you to pay attention to them once again. But stay committed and don't give in!

What if too few people "Make the Cut"? How do you go about making new acquaintances? Start spending more time with the people whose names are on the right. Take part in whatever activities they are doing, including clubs, study sessions, sports, and volunteering. This will give you access to their networks. In due time, you'll have replaced your former team of naysayers, instigators, and perpetrators, with a slew of creators, activators, and motivators.

Motivators, not haters

Always stay positive. The second you allow your positive state of mind to be stolen by the people who criticize you or diminish your accomplishments, you've lost control. Teenagers can be very jealous and vindictive. As an assistant principal, I had to deal with cars scratched, egged, and vandalized with obscene messages. I also had to deal with electronic harassment, for example, untraceable apps being used to message foul words to a person. There are just some people in this world that can't stand seeing others succeed. You know them as "haters."

Take the "hating" as a sign. You must be doing something right if others are giving you negative attention despite your many accomplishments. It means you have a big fan base that's spread the word about how great you are, and reached the ear of some person(s) who don't agree. You should be proud you're getting "hated on." I've worked with many teens that became so wrapped up in trying to please everyone. They'd go to great lengths to make sure a "hater" was happy, like being incredibly nice even when the "hater" didn't deserve it. I learned one valuable lesson from my ten years as an administrator: You can't please everybody. Someone will always find fault in you or in your actions.

Don't waste time and energy attempting to please everybody. If a "friend" ever tells you someone doesn't like you, please don't ever let this come out of your mouth: "Why?" Or worse: "What did I do?" Here's how you should respond instead: "I don't have time for haters." Or better still: "Haters are my motivators." And why shouldn't they be? The negativity from haters is useful. Provided they aren't attempting to bully you, you should use haters as fuel to make you work even harder. Correcting your actions in response to meritless comments about you is stepping back; it is like retreating. Successful people stop, and even adjust their course, but they never retreat. They keep moving forward.

Remember that the only opinion of you that really matters is your own. What I've found is that the teens that pay the most attention to the opinions of "haters" have the lowest opinion of themselves (self-esteem). If you struggle with your self-esteem, a great self-help book to read is, *The Self-Esteem Workbook for Teens: Activities to Help You Build*

Confidence and Achieve Your Goals, by Lisa M. Schab LCSW.

True friendships take many years to establish. The word, "friend," is used far too lightly by many of you. You call every kid you hang out with at school your friend. This can be a big mistake. Successful people don't form false friendship bonds with everyone they interact with. Successful people instead are very selective when promoting an acquaintance to the status of friend. If you are to be successful, you need to do the same. Finally, successful people know when to terminate a friendship. When is that? As soon as a friend breaks laws, becomes emotionally dependent on you, or tries to pull you down instead of uplift you. Pay special attention to who you run with, or risk getting run over.

Chapter 5 Main Points:

1. Friendships take years to form. Unless you grew up as children with someone at your school, most of the people you call your friends are actually acquaintances.
2. Be especially careful about how you choose your acquaintances at school. If they discourage hard work, commitment to your responsibilities, personal growth, or making good choices, they are NOT your friends, or even worth keeping as acquaintances.
3. Allowing "haters" to get in your head is a warning sign that perhaps you're self-esteem is low. "Haters" can be motivators if you use their negative energy to fuel your inner fire to succeed.

Chapter 6
You're An Idiot As Long As You Think You Are

This is the story of a prophet that spoke to me when I was fourteen. In, "Three types of people," from Chapter 1, I mentioned that I started to hang out with more scholarly students during 9th grade. I had one friend in particular in my new circle of "friends" that was incredibly smart. The worst part about it, he knew it. He'd assert his dominance over the rest of us with his superior smarts. Trying to argue with him was pointless. He wouldn't stop talking until he proved his ideas right, and everyone else's wrong. If it weren't for the fact that he was extremely loyal, funny, and giving, I may not have continued spending time with him.

Do you know someone that doesn't need to study to pull an "A" in all of their math tests? Someone who is perhaps in the gifted and talented program? These types of teenagers don't do their homework ever, earn just barely above average grades, rudely challenge their teachers often in the middle of class, and yet still earn a National Merit Scholarship because of great S.A.T scores. That was my friend, Malik (not his real name). Malik and I had many things in common. We both obsessed about racism and the oppression of minorities by whites.

We both disliked our fathers. His mother and father were separated. We were both members of the track team, and loved to compete. We also loved to eat *carne asada* burritos and homemade oatmeal cookies.

Malik had a bad habit of calling people idiots, especially me. Every time I'd say something dumb in conversation, jokingly or not, he'd say, "You're an idiot, Los." My first name is Carlos and people called me, "Los." Coming from him, those words had a huge impact on my self-esteem. Maybe I am an idiot? I'd say to myself. He's clearly some sort of genius, and I'm not. I was of average of intelligence and Malik was born with better genetics. This is seriously how flawed my thinking was back then.

Your brainpower isn't capped

I remember the first time I went over Malik's house as if it were yesterday. He lived in a modest North San Jose three bedroom, one bath home with his mother, older sister, and a few pets. He led me to his room, and opened the door. "Man, you're messy," I said to him, noticing dirty dishes, and a bunch of clothes on top of his bed and on the floor. Having never had a bedroom of my own to keep tidy, it was shocking seeing Malik's room look as if a tornado had blown through. After the initial shock, I took a closer look across Malik's room and saw something that blew my mind: a huge stack of books!

"What are you doing with all them books?" I asked Malik. "Oh," he said, "we don't have cable TV and my mom buys me books to read." His mom buys him books? I thought to myself. What kind of mom buys books for their son? "She's a middle school teacher," Malik said. I was numb. This moment was a powerful revelation because it meant that Malik wasn't genetically superior to me. He'd just read way more books than I had, and his mom had probably helped him learn better in elementary and middle school. My mom wasn't going to help me learn; she hadn't even graduated from middle school in Mexico. But I could sure help myself by reading a lot more.

This whole time I was under the spell of a false belief that intelligence is God-given. God is great and almighty, but not limiting! "Look," said Malik. "This is the book I'm currently reading." In his hand was a copy of The Prophet by Kahlil Gibran. The book's cover image was that of a man's face drawn in pencil. The shading around the eyes of this thinly mustached man gave him a penetrating gaze. Whoever this was, I felt as if he were staring at my soul, and telling it to seek peace from wisdom.

In her best-selling book, Mindset: The New Psychology of Success, Dr. Carol S. Dweck explains that there are two types of people, those with a "fixed mindset," and those with a "growth mindset." People with a fixed mindset have self-limiting beliefs about their abilities and talents.

What are self-limiting beliefs? Self-limiting beliefs are things you believe about you that place a limit on your abilities. Sometimes you're not even aware you have these beliefs.

Each year I teach physics to eighth graders. When I tell them that there will be more math, someone always yells, "But I suck at math, Homie G!" This is a clear example of both a limiting belief and a fixed mindset. I then ask, "Why do you suck at math"? The usual response is, "I don't know. I just don't get it." Telling your teachers you "don't get it" doesn't help much by the way. You have to be more specific and clear when you communicate. For example, "I need more help when solving for variables." Now your teacher feels empowered to take action and assist you because they have a skill they can target.

I happen to know why many of you "suck" at math. For starters, you don't believe you can get better at it. Perhaps some of your teachers and experiences have wrongly taught you that math is a subject that you either get, or you don't. And because you believe that your brainpower in math is capped, meaning with no more room to expand, you fail to do the one thing that would make you better at math: practice. Practicing is what makes you great at video games, dancing, or sports. It's the same with math.

You can't expect to do math only at school and be good at it. You must practice doing math after school at least one hour a day. No way! That's what you just thought, isn't it? Okay then continue sucking at math. Unfortunately, math happens to be one of the biggest gatekeepers holding teens of color back from getting accepted to college. And it doesn't have to be! So please do yourself a huge favor and practice enough hours to pass your high school math classes with excellent grades.

A person with a growth mindset understands that success in any activity is tied to hard work, persistence, and dedication. Growth mindset individuals are not afraid of a challenge because failing to try means automatically failing. Meanwhile, actually trying a challenge means there is at least a possibility of success, even if it happens to be a small one. Growth mindset individuals also add one key word at the end of ability limiting sentences that set them apart from self-limiting people: "yet." See examples below.

Fixed Mindset	Growth Mindset
I can't do algebra 1.	I can't do algebra 1, yet.
I don't understand chemistry.	I don't understand chemistry, yet.
I'm not good at basketball.	I'm not good at basketball, yet.
I'm not a good dancer.	I'm not a good dancer, yet.
I can't talk to girls.	I can't talk to girls, yet.

The good news is that you can replace a fixed mindset with a growth mindset. It won't take a powerful revelation like the type I had many years ago in Malik's room. It's actually quite simple to adopt a growth mindset.

Time, patience, and positive affirmations

You talk to yourself, right? Yeah, so do I. In fact, we all do. That voice in your head can be a great companion in your life's journey or an awful one. Who have you been letting ride beside you? Many of you have given control of your journey's steering wheel to an impatient, negative, and speedy jerk. You must watch what your inner voice says. As humans, our brains are programmed (via DNA) to listen to the words of others. It increases our chances of survival. We call it our sense of hearing. In this hyper stressful day and age, you have to extend your sense of hearing to include listening to your inner voice. Without fear, you need to confront your inner voice every time it speaks with a fixed mindset. Start doing this now!

Positive affirmations, nice things you can say to yourself daily, are one way to challenge and weaken that jerk that's taken over your head. Below are some creative positive affirmations I say to myself to this day. They have been tweaked over time.

My potential is as limitless as the universe.
I inspire people to inspire themselves.
My energy is more contagious than Ebola.
My hard work eats smart things for breakfast, lunch, and dinner.
The bigger the hill is, the better my view at the top.
I'm like a rubber ball; I can bounce back from anything.

Famous people also lived (or live) by affirmations of their own. See for yourself:

"It's not that I'm smart, it's just that I stay with problems longer."
Albert Einstein

"I've failed over and over and over again in my life...and that is why I succeed."
Michael Jordan

"If you hear a voice within you say, 'you cannot paint,' then by all means paint, and that voice will be silenced."
Vincent Van Gogh

"To hell with circumstances; I create opportunities."
Bruce Lee

"It does not matter how slowly you go so long as you do not stop."
Confucius

Growth Mindset Exercise:

For this exercise, you will need at least five, 3 x 5 cards. If you don't have cards, then a piece of paper will do. Get on the Internet. Google: "Growth Mindset Affirmations." Now hit the "Images" tab at the top. You will see an entire page full of pictures of growth mindset affirmations.

Spend a few minutes looking at all of the pictures. Whenever you come across an affirmation that you like, write it down on a 3 x 5 card or your piece of paper. Do this until you have at least five done. For five months straight, say these affirmations to yourself whenever you catch your inner voice speaking fixed mindset language. Did you just say, "That's a long time," to yourself? I read your mind. Make it six months straight! I also want you to say these affirmations at least one time in front of the mirror each morning. If you "forget," then do it in the afternoon or evening before going to bed. No excuses.

You'll need to carry these affirmations everywhere you go. If you're better with technology, you can transfer these onto your Notes app on your smartphone. You can even create a growth mindset board on Pinterest and pin as many of those images as you want. It takes time and patience to replace a negative inner voice. You owe it to yourself to take all the time you need to succeed in this undertaking. Be patient, it will happen.

I'm not and never was an idiot or stupid. Malik almost succeeded in making me believe I was. After learning his secret, I never again questioned the limit of my intelligence. I have proven to myself over and over that no matter how far back I am, or think I am, I can always catch up. If you put forth the effort, nothing is out of reach.

If you're wondering, Malik and I are still friends. Today, Malik is a medical doctor and delivers babies for a living.

Chapter 6 Main Points:

1. People fail to try because of their self-limiting beliefs about their abilities and talents. Failing to try is automatically failing and a sure way of never succeeding.
2. People with a growth mindset believe their ability to learn isn't limited. They know that patience, persistence, and positive affirmations are the keys to learning anything.

Chapter 7
Don't Waste Time Fighting Your Identity Challengers

In the last chapter I mentioned that people called me, "Los," in high school. I actually had two other nicknames. They were, "C-los," and "C-Mex." "C-los," was yet another shortening of my first name. "C-Mex," on the other hand, was an abbreviation that had to do with my identity. It stood for Carlos for Mexicans. Of all the things I protected from others, for example, my residency status, the pain of being made to feel worthless by my father, my lack of confidence with girls, and the suspicions about my intelligence, there was one thing I protected above all else: my ethnic identity.

I could hide everything else, but not how I looked. I was (and still am) a fair-skinned Latino. As a young man I used to wish I had been born darker. My skin color was the biggest contradiction in my life. I felt like I had to prove who I was to everyone. "You're Mexican?" kids I'd meet would ask. After saying a few things in Spanish as proof they'd say, "Well, you look white." Hearing this dozens of times made me feel very insecure.

I got totally fed up with it, and decided I'd create a mask to hide this insecurity about my identity. I started calling myself, "C-Mex, defender of

Mexican rights." I had to be the most Mexican person at my school. I pinned a small Mexican flag to my backpack. In classes, I'd interrupt lessons by yelling what Mexican people accomplished. My teachers would tell me to go stand outside.

In Math I'd say, "The Mayans invented the concept of zero!" In history I'd say, "The U.S. stole California, Nevada, New Mexico, Arizona, and parts of Texas from Mexico!" In science I'd say, "Mexicans invented modern chewing gum!" Word of my overbearing pride soon spread and the nickname, C-Mex, stuck. My new super-Mexican identity came at a huge cost. I lost hours of learning time waiting for my teacher to come talk to me outside of the classroom. I also had to have a strong "comeback" every time a "friend" from another ethnic group made a Mexican joke. In other words, I had to constantly "represent." Becoming C-Mex burdened me even more.

Don't let others give you identity insecurity

From having been a teen, and also from having worked in schools for over 16 years, I know each of you has some sort of identity insecurity. You're still trying to find yourself. Let me tell you that you still have a long way to go and that's okay. Because your identity is in this vulnerable stage though, it's easy for others to push your buttons. If you're an ethnically mixed person, other students of color may never truly accept you as one of their own. If you're fair-skinned, then you won't be dark enough to darker members of your ethnic group. If you should have friends that are not members of the ethnic group you belong to, you'll be considered a sell-out. If you're too dark, members of your own ethnic group will call you names. There is no end to how petty and mean kids can be to each other.

Always be proud of who you are and the way you look. Your looks make you unique and that's all. They don't disqualify you in any way from how you identify ethnically. The ethnic group(s) you identify with because of your heritage are entirely up to you, not someone else. I made the mistake of allowing others to put me in conflict with my own self-image. What was the result? I used up valuable mental energy constantly proving who I was to my identity challengers. These identity haters played with my emotions, and it was my own fault because I allowed them to.

How can you keep from becoming insecure about your ethnicity? Below are five realizations that calmed my insecurity and finally allowed me to focus on my educational goals.

- Everyone is made up of genes from multiple ethnic groups.

- There is no single representation of a culture.

- The large sums of money I'll make one day won't care what my ethnicity is.

- There are many others who look just like me.

- Every kid at my school is working on their identity as well.

If you've shamed someone else for not falling within your standards of ethnicity, ask yourself this question right now: Why am I doing this? If the answer doesn't hit you right away, come back to the question later.

But be sure to keep at it until you identify the source of this emotional problem. Also ask yourself this question next: How would it make me feel if someone questioned who I was once, twice, even several times? You must understand that people who are successful don't waste time judging others by their looks or ethnic backgrounds. Successful people come in all shapes, sizes, and colors!

You're not selling out, you're selling in

One of the biggest insults I got back in school was being called a sell-out. It didn't happen often, but when it did, I couldn't let it go. I had to dish it right back to the person or risk being labeled a sissy. I should've just ignored the fools calling me a sell-out, but the "street" in me made me reactive.

What is reactive? Reactive people are the type to become defensive or protective when challenged. They can't help fighting fire with fire.

In some schools, the street mentality is hard to escape because reactive people are everywhere. But escape you must if you're to be successful in life.
I noticed that the more academic I became, meaning, nerdy, the more my "friends" would poke fun at me. I started taking tougher classes after my freshman year of high school. These included English honors, Algebra 2, Biology, Chemistry, Physics, and AP Art History. As I climbed the academic ladder, I left behind acquaintances and even family members. My older sister struggled in high school, and had to finish her education at a continuation high school. She was not dumb or lazy; she just didn't connect with the school system. Sadly,

attending continuation high school is the fate of many students in this country who can't click with school.

While I was at UC Santa Barbara, I had very little time for my older sister. I missed her tremendously. When I would return back home to San Jose, I could tell things between her and I were not the same. We both had changed and grown apart. I became a critic of her lifestyle. She had chosen to get married young and have kids. She was having a hard time being a young mother and keeping a full time job. My mother had to step in and help my older sister get through each week. Naturally, I didn't like this arrangement. My mother would often complain openly about how irresponsible my older sister was behaving.

At family gatherings, my older sister and I would take turns taking sides if either of us challenged our parents' worldview. If my mother started lecturing my sister, I'd jump in anytime my sister started ignoring her. "Pay attention!" I'd say to her. Of course my older sister had her own way of getting even. If I challenged my mom's unscientific suggestions or explanations with what I'd learned in college, my sister would say to me, "Okay, *Profe*!" sarcastically. "Profe" was short for the word, professor. She meant that I was acting uppity and needed to tone it down.

Have family members mocked you for sounding smart? Have kids at school ever said that you're "acting white" or are "whitewashed" because of how you speak? I was really offended when my sister called me, *Profe*, so I can imagine how you have felt if this has happened to you. It's discouraging, especially when it comes from your own family. I also felt like I was betraying my own people. I felt so guilty that when I left for UC Santa Barbara I listened to

Mexican music the entire drive there. I was leaving behind my close-knit family, my *hood*, and my *homies*.

I'm incredibly glad that I decided to sell-in to this other world. Yes it's dominated by white people, but it's not exclusive to whites. There are so many more successful people of color these days. People like Daymond John, Jennifer Lopez, Pitbull, Dr. Dre, and Jessica Alba are millionaire entrepreneurs known for creating valuable brands. They're just a few examples of the thousands of people of color who have reached the top of their industries following success principles. As younger versions of themselves, they no doubt had identity challenges and insecurities like everyone else. These successful people of color have paved the way for many aspiring entrepreneurs of color. Yes, someday you can be like them.

The good news is that as you become more focused on your success, and stay committed, you'll wear out all of your identity critics. Eventually those around you will see that you are, as they say, "for reals," about making it big. They'll begin to respect what you're doing for yourself or for your family. Keep those you love, including yourself, in the front of your mind whenever your identity is tested by others. Even if it's your own family that's discouraging you, leaving them temporarily to go off to college or avoiding them to keep your mindset positive, is how you show them that you love them. Because once you become successful, you'll be in a better position to help out.

Chapter 7 Main Points:

1. Your ethnic identity is in a process of constant change; you're insecure about it if you are reactive.
2. To avoid being reactive when your ethnic identity is tested, keep in mind that we all have multiple ethnic groups in our heritage, there's no one single representation of a culture, there are many that look just like you, success and money are colorblind, and kids at your school are also working on their identity.
3. Don't feel guilty about leaving anyone behind, including your friends, family, and even community, as you climb the success ladder. Sell-in all the way. As a successful adult you'll be in a better position to help others.

Chapter 8
Be A Master Of Accountability Not A Slave Of Blame

I watched too much television as an adolescent and teen. Cable TV had just come out, and channel surfing became the new American hobby. My favorite time to watch television was during the winter holidays. Major television networks would have classic movies showing from Halloween all the way to New Year's Day. Some of my favorite classic movies were, The Wizard of Oz, The Sound of Music, Willy Wonka & the Chocolate Factory, and The Ten Commandments. Out of all of these, The Ten Commandments taught me the most about success.

The Ten Commandments is the story of Moses, played by actor Charlton Heston, and the liberation of the Hebrew slaves from Pharaoh Rameses, played by actor Yul Brynner. There are plenty of lessons to highlight from this epic bible tale. However, I'm going to share the one that was most mind-altering to me in my youth. Before watching this movie, I was a typical teen, cheating my way through school. I copied people's homework, cut corners while running laps around the field in P.E., didn't finish class projects, and even cheated on tests.

This movie taught me the significance and meaning of accountability. What is accountability?

Because I love business so much, I will give you a business definition:

Accountability: *noun*: The obligation of an individual or organization to account for its activities, accept responsibility for them, and to disclose the results in a transparent manner. It also includes the responsibility for money or other entrusted property. *Source: BusinessDictionary.com*

I wasn't taking care of business when it came to my personal character. When I viewed both Moses and Pharaoh being accountable for their promises and to their people, I practically lost it. How could anyone hold themselves to such high ethical standards? I thought. I was puny in comparison. When I was accused of starting trouble in class, I'd point the finger at someone else. The same thing happened at home. When I'd forget to do a chore my father instructed me to do, I'd come up with an excuse or blame my older sister.

Some things *were* my fault. I just had a hard time facing the lack of accountability I had for myself. While watching The Ten Commandments I came upon a mind hack that would push me to be more accountable. There is a famous line in the movie that gets repeated by the opposing characters of Moses and Pharaoh. It is: "So let it be written, so let it be done." I loved this line! To me it meant that if something is going to get done, it had better be already written down in the history books as an accomplishment. In other words, in the Egyptian culture of ancient times, if Pharaoh commands something in a certain way, his historians better write it as such, and his subjects better get it done as written; Pharaoh's great legacy is literally etched in stone. Now that's accountability!

I liked, "So let it be written, so let it be done," so much I started using it as my own catch phrase at school. Other kids thought I was weird. My track coach and teachers were impressed. If they asked me to do something, I'd say the line and act as if it was already done. Of course it meant that I actually had to produce, and not just run my mouth. How are you keeping yourself accountable? If you're not holding yourself accountable, you absolutely must change this about yourself. No one will trust you if you can't keep your word. Not keeping your word or promises, and not having something to stand for, makes you a person without integrity.

Successful people are first and foremost leaders who are accountable to themselves and their employees. Successful people know that whatever they commit to doing or instruct others to do, must get done. Their businesses or brands are penalized financially if there is no accountability, and workers do whatever they want. Below is a strategy you can use to up your accountability.

Make A Bet Exercise:

Students your age love to make bets. This exercise gives you permission to make bets with others all the time. If you are assigned something to do by your teacher or parents, think how you can turn completing the task into a small wager. For example, let's say you have to make a Google slides presentation on a given topic and it's due in a week.

Find a classmate in the same class and tell them that you will pay them $10 if you don't get it done one day before it's due. Share the document with them as proof when you've met your deadline. Here's another example. Say your parents notice you have an F in Math. Apologize to them for not being accountable. Once you're done apologizing, bet them a whole month of doing the dishes every evening if you don't raise your grade to at least a C- by the next progress report.

The key is to get creative with your bets and to risk losing something of value to you, for example, your time or money, if you should lose the bet. I guarantee that by doing this exercise your accountability will be more important to you than ever before.

Why you're a savage when it comes to blame

Many of you are hyper-sensitive to blame. As an educator, I've seen first-hand how you react when being blamed. To put it nicely, you can't handle it. What do cats do when they get ready to fight? They arch their backs and puff their hair to appear bigger. That's how many of you respond when your teachers or parents blame you for anything. You get super defensive, raising and changing the tone of your voice. To deflect the blame you either come up with an excuse or you blame someone else.

Why are you a savage when it comes to blame? Is it because you are innocent all the time and you're just defending yourself from your accusers? You may have not been responsible for *all* the things you have been accused of doing, but I'm confident that you have been responsible for *some* things. Just like I was. In truth, the reason you get so worked up when someone blames you is because you have been over blamed.

It's very easy to assign someone or something else blame. Most adults in this country have relied on blame all of their lives to explain their failures. If they have a job and life they hate, they blame the poor education they got at school, their parents for messing them up as children, or their own kids for forcing them to be responsible adults. Kids become targets of blame at a young age. At first, they allow the adult to blame them, staying quiet. But once they get older, kids learn that making excuses or blaming someone else is how you deal with blame.

Teenagers I've known blamed their parents for "ruining" their lives. Your life doesn't even really begin until you graduate from high school. But if you're already casting blame on your parents, your life will suck because the cycle of blame has been officially passed down to you. You will move from blaming your parents to blaming your future bosses, teachers, professors, the weather, the dog, and on and on.

You must stop reacting like a savage when being blamed, especially at school where you will always lose against the adults. There are better ways to respond to blame without getting on the offensive. Below are some suggestions I've given students.

If you get blamed for something, even if it wasn't your fault, you must not fight the accusation out loud. Adults, especially teachers, will consider this a classroom disruption and may write you up. When it's more convenient, approach your teacher and give them the truth. Explain to them why you weren't at fault. If you were at fault, apologize to them and let them know that you will be more accountable for your behavior starting immediately. If talking to your teacher in private scares you, get over it. You have to learn to stick up for yourself. You will also be separating yourself from the crowd when you treat your accountability as something of value you don't want tarnished. Trust me the adults will notice.

If you're constantly blamed at home by angry and frustrated parents who need you to be their "bad guy" so they can handle life, ask yourself these questions: Am I really this bad person? What does my heart have to say about me? The answers to these questions will either confirm or deny what your parents think of you. How will you correct your behavior and show your parents more accountability if you are being "bad"? My advice is for you to be a master of accountability one day at a time until you restore your parent's trust in you.

How will you deal with parents who blame you unfairly all the time? After all, you learned in Chapter 3 that you can't change who your parents are. I suggest you find a place in your heart to forgive your parents and respectfully dismiss their blame. Forgiving isn't easy; it requires know-how. A great place to start learning how to forgive is Robert D. Enright's book, *Forgiveness is a Choice: A Step-by-Step Process for Resolving Anger and Restoring Hope.* Check it out at your local branch library.

Personal accountability is a requirement of success. It's also how you can tell the difference between good leaders and great ones. Moses and Pharaoh were great leaders and models of accountability. The time has come for you to be accountable and a role model to others. Never again let anyone have to hold you accountable. From now on, it's your job. So let it be written, so let it be done.

Chapter 8 Main Points:

1. Your personal character is the most valuable possession you have.
2. There is nothing more important to your personal character than maintaining your integrity and accountability.
3. Being over-blamed in your life is not an excuse to continue the practice of blaming things or others for your failures. Be careful how you react when being blamed; it gives people a bad impression of you when you react like a savage.

Chapter 9
You're Right, School Does Suck

Your school sucks, and so do most public schools in this country. How I see it, only a handful of schools across the nation (those offering trade, technical, or technological skill certificates) are preparing you for the real world. But isn't that what schools are supposed to be doing? That's what many, especially high schools, say they do. But it's all a lie. Many of you already know that. That's why you have such a hard time staying motivated to take school seriously or even to attend.

I had the great fortune of attending an engineering magnet high school. Aside from college prep courses, I took electives in drafting (with Computer Aided Design), Electronics, and Metal shop. I even got to stay one week at the University of Santa Clara to learn the latest in engineering and computers. I sent my first email across the world to a pen pal in Australia in 1992! Computer monitors were the size of 32-inch televisions (not the flat screen type) back then. Living in Silicon Valley, I could've focused on Information Technology (I-T for short) in Junior College and have done very well for myself professionally, but only because I was exposed to these real world application classes in high school.

Sadly, skills courses vanished for a long time, replaced by more English, Math, History, and

Science. Not to mention wave after wave of state tests most of you hate taking. Skills courses are finally making a comeback. Why? Educators and politicians realized how important these subjects are in today's day and age. Skill classes have been rebranded by the education system as Science, Technology, Engineering, and Math or S.T.E.M. It's given some kids a reason to get excited about school again. Having robotics, coding, digital and media design, and any elective that provides digital badges of certification get you even closer to learning the stuff of the 21st Century. I'd still like to see the trades make a full comeback. We'll always need plumbers, electricians, carpenters, and to some degree, auto mechanics.

Your teachers sell one product, and you're not buying it

Teachers, counselors, principals, they're all obsessed. They're obsessed with pushing college on every kid that walks inside a school campus. Some kids don't even make it past second grade before some adult starts brainwashing them about going to college. These adults mean well. After all, college graduates do *make* more money *on average* than those with only a high school diploma or a vocational certificate. But there are also plenty of reasons why going to a four-year college after high school doesn't make sense for many teenagers. Which teenagers should reconsider enrolling in a four-year college even if accepted? See my list below:

1. You don't have a clear idea of what you want to major in. Don't let your pushy teachers convince you to attend an expensive university

with a reason like, "You got two years to declare a major...don't worry it'll come to you, just go."

2. You know what you want to major in, but it falls in the "Least Valuable College Majors" category. Last time I checked, some of the worst college majors for your time and money include anthropology, archeology, film, photography, fine arts, philosophy, religious studies, liberal arts, music, physical fitness, history, and English literature.

3. You don't have a career in mind. Going to college is not a right of passage into adulthood, as many kids believe. You don't go to college for the experience it provides. You go because you want to learn theoretical and practical knowledge that transfers directly to a career.

Many students of color don't like school. I talked to hundreds of them as a high school assistant principal. "Why don't you like school?" I'd ask them. Their usual response was, "It's boring." Is this how *you* feel about school? What these students were telling me was that what they were being offered as learning didn't have any connection to their heart or mind. What they were being taught didn't make any sense to them. Schools also suck then because they too often offer the same type of education for every student. All kids are different, especially when it comes to their interests and personal learning style. So why do schools try to teach every pupil the same? College. The programs, the teaching, the counseling, it's all designed to graduate students, college ready.

So you too don't like school. Now what? Can't think of anything? Let Homie G give you some advice. First, you must graduate from high school. I don't care what it takes for you to have to do this. If you've dug yourself a deep hole, failing a bunch of classes, stop digging. Pass all of your classes from now on. Easy for me to say, right? Stop thinking of excuses! Next, take credit recovery classes until you have earned the credits needed to get back on pace to graduate.

Graduating from high school is a big deal. Many of you will be the first in your family to do this. Being able to "walk" at graduation is a privilege your guardians will want you to earn. Your efforts are not just for you. They're for all that family that would love nothing more than to see you one day in a cap and gown.

What happens after high school? After high school you have the following options:

1. Find a job and go to work. If you're lucky, a family member will take you under their wing and give you a job, or a job lead. Otherwise you can look for a low-level entry job like working at a fast food restaurant.

2. Start your own job. Beg your family and friends for some start-up money to get your small business going. I can't imagine your high school preparing you to be an entrepreneur so if you go this route, more power to you.

3. Enroll at a trade school or become an apprentice. You may just be gifted with your hands and becoming a carpenter,

electrician, mechanic, plumber, or handyman is what you were born to do.

4. Sit at home and do nothing. This one may not go so well with your parents or guardians.

Graduating high school with better grades gives you two additional options. You can enroll at a 2-year or a 4-year college. I'll explain later why I prefer you enroll at a 2-year college over going straight to a 4-year college. For now, let's talk about grades.

Don't fall in love with grades, fall in love with effort

The public believes that schools in the United States are college preparation factories. Not true. They're college *acceptance* factories. Big difference. According to the National Assessment of Educational Progress, also known as the Nation's Report Card, only about one-third of high school seniors were prepared for college-level coursework in math and reading in 2015. What this means is that 66% of high school seniors have done everything according to plan, keeping great attendance, behavior, and grades but still aren't college ready. That's a lot of unprepared kids. I was one of them in the mid '90s.

I graduated high school with a 3.33 grade point average. I took many honors and even some Advanced Placement classes. I thought I was a big deal when I set foot at San Jose City College until I got my first graded college essay returned to me. I scored a "D" on my first English 101 writing assignment. I couldn't believe it. Here I thought I was a great writer. My high school English teachers never gave me less than a "B." This professor had marked up my paper with her red pen. I didn't even know where to begin looking at it.

I thought I had perhaps not given the essay assignment the attention it deserved. So for the second one, I really took my time and gave it everything I had. The result? I got a stinking "C-." You can't spend a lot of time in college complaining about the results of your grades. You're paying for classes so failing them is a waste of both your time and money. I decided I needed help. There was more to the skill of writing that I had not learned in high school. Luckily, there was a writing lab on campus. I spent a couple of hours each day working with the teaching assistants until my writing improved. My efforts paid off. I went on to earn "B's" and "A's" on future English assignments and passed the course.

So here's the moral of the story: high school gives you a false sense of subject or skill mastery. Getting above average grades means nothing in college where you'll need to prove yourself once again. Many of you are caught in the lie that having excellent grades makes you smart or capable. Not so. Having stellar grades makes you at most a stellar student. And to disappoint you even more, being a top student at your school doesn't mean you'd be one somewhere else. Many of you are in a fish bowl believing your school is the best place to swim on the planet. You don't see that there are thousands of schools like yours (or better) across America. Each high school in the U.S. has one valedictorian at graduation and there are over 21,000 public and 10,000 private high schools!

Get over being in love with your grades. It's great that you have earned them but realize that they're not a true measure of your abilities. As an educator I can tell you that the grades you earn are based on multiple useless factors like your citizenship, homework, and classwork. They may also be influenced by how your teacher feels on any given day, and the academic level of the other students in your classes. When a student brags about his or her grades to me I always ask them this question: "Compared to whom?" They usually have no idea what I'm talking about so I add this: "You mean compared to the other kids at this school you're happy with the grades you got?" Then they say, "Yeah." I have to then break it down for them, "But you're not competing in life just with the kids at this school. You're up against every other kid your age in this country." The look on their face is of shock and defeat.

Successful people get fired up knowing they're challenging every other person in their generation. The numbers don't scare them. The more people they have to beat, the sweeter the victories. Successful people know that most people are lazy, lack focus, and have no idea of the amount of effort it takes to be at the top. They love feats that take incredible effort because very few people are willing to do them. That's how successful people stay ahead, working harder than everyone.

So instead of being proud of your grades you should be most proud of your efforts. If a student in your class earns an "A" purposely doing the least amount of work, and you earn the same grade working your tail off, who is winning? You're learning the role of effort in life and they're not, so you're beating them. No matter the outcome you always have to put forth 100% effort. Since college preparedness isn't a guaranteed outcome of your high school education, you must from here on out put forth double the effort to make up the shortfall. I'll show you how in the next chapter.

Chapter 9 Main Points:

1. You're right to not trust your school. Most of them aren't preparing you for the real world; they're trying to get you accepted to college. This doesn't sound so bad until you realize most high schools fail to get students college-ready.
2. Enrolling in a four-year college may not be your best option, even if you got accepted to your first choice.
3. Not graduating from high school, or graduating with poor grades, limits the options you'll have once you're on your own.
4. Even if you're the top of your class you shouldn't be content with your grades. Grades mean very little in the grand scheme of things.

Chapter 10
Twice The Effort In The Same Amount of Time

Wouldn't it be great if we didn't have to sleep? Just imagine how many more things we could get done in a 24-hour day if we didn't have to get rest. Honestly, I think most people would just spend more time doing things that don't contribute to their success with those extra seven to eight hours. They'd be watching more sports on TV, eating, playing X-box, scrolling on their phone, and so on. I have figured out how to make more time out of my day and devote those extra precious hours toward fulfilling my goals.

I've never been one to carry an agenda or a to-do list. In fact, I hate those two particular types of time management strategies. They used to give me a false sense of productivity. This is back when I thought being productive was getting a bunch of random things done. Because I'm goal oriented now, I can concentrate all day on just two to three things I need to do. I use the time driving to and from work, walking at school, working out, regular and bathroom breaks, and while I'm with my kids sometimes, to do something that contributes to building my success. Unlike most people, I don't need breaks and I don't have to relax when I get home. I may spend 2 hours a week watching TV and 1 hour a week on my phone.

In contrast, I spend about 12 hours a week reading, and at least 10 hours a week writing. Like all successful people, I place a high value on my time.

From the previous paragraph you should have gathered that how you choose to spend your time is vital. Are you stopping to think before you choose to do something? Or are you just reacting to whatever comes your way? You have more time on hand than you think. For example, instead of hanging out after school you could be reading. Instead of playing outdoors you could be reading. Instead of jumping on your PS4 as soon as you get home you could be reading. Reading? Now there's an idea.

You don't read enough and you don't even know it

When students tell me, "I don't like to read," I tell them, "Well do you like to be broke"? It's that simple, readers are leaders. You have no idea how much reading you should be doing. You should be reading at least one book a week. The book must be at your reading level or one level above. If you stick to this pace, you'll read 52 books a year. Now that's a great feat.

Some of you may read every day, but you're reading books that'll never make you any money. Before I write about the types of books you should be reading outside of your school day, let's figure out how to make more time. Here are some suggestions on how to make more time for reading:

1) Go to bed early. Set your alarm to wake-up one hour earlier than your usual time. Read while everyone else sleeps so you are not distracted.

2) Get your exercise during P.E. This means going as hard as you can during class. If you don't tire yourself out during P.E. you won't be getting enough physical activity for the day.

3) Don't do club sports. It's not enough for many of you to do a school sport after school. Some of you play year round, paying to participate as part of a club team. You better be a great, and I mean, great, athlete if you're playing year round.

4) Keep your room or area where you sleep at home neat and tidy. Dumping your dirty clothes, trash, or gear wherever will tie you up later longer than necessary when your parents force you to clean.

5) Use the dead time many of your teachers leave at the end of the period for you to pack up to do homework from other classes. Don't waste the time chatting with kids in the class or standing at the door. This way you'll have less homework to do later.

6) Go to the library during lunch (after you've eaten) and do homework you've been assigned. If you don't have homework, great! Now you are free to spend the time reading.

7) Spend less time in front of the mirror putting on make-up or grooming. Unless you plan on going to beauty school or being a model, you shouldn't be obsessed with your appearance.

8) Don't kill time watching YouTube videos, playing against people online with your game console, or listening to music. Listen to audiobooks or podcasts instead.

Can you think of any other wasteful activities to get rid of from your day-to-day life?

As you can see, none of those things are easy and they all involve you giving up something. This is called making sacrifices. If you're truly serious about becoming a success, you must be self-disciplined with your time so you can get twice the Profitable Action done on any given day. The Profitable Action is twofold because you're not only handling every thing your teachers throw your way, which isn't enough to prepare you for the real world or even college most of the time, but you're also working on your SMART goals. I know what you're thinking: *But I'll have no life*. You'll have a great life! In the future. While everyone else will be struggling, you'll be thriving.

Time management strategies of the highly successful

How do successful people make sure to get to their daily goals and find time to read? They use a couple of time management strategies. The first one is simple. Successful people prioritize. They have plenty of things to choose from to do on any given day, just like everyone else. Unlike everyone else, they choose to do only those few things that relate directly to their goals and success. You have too many priorities in your life, too many masters of your time. You have let your various priorities organize and structure you, instead of the other way around.

Prioritizing then, is actively thinking about your day the night before and crossing off things on your plate that kill time. Once you've trimmed your day, you then have to number what's left from 1 to 5. See the example below.

My Priorities for (Date)

1. Go to school and get all my work done as efficiently as possible.
2. Exercise at least 1 hour. P.E. counts for about _____ minutes, not including the time I spend dressing out or dressing back into my clothes.
3. Read my "success" book for 1-hour.
4. Practice doing my hobby or thing I'm most passionate about for 1-hour.
5. Skype or meet with my success motivated friends for 30 minutes to discuss our goals and brainstorm how to overcome current challenges.

The second time management strategy successful people use is creating daily schedules. This involves you writing down your priorities next to the time you will actually be doing them. Have you ever heard adults say, "Let me look at my schedule"? All highly effective professionals have a schedule. This keeps non-emergency events from interrupting and taking over their day. You'll have a difficult time of getting to your prioritized activities if you don't 1) schedule them, 2) follow your schedule, and 3) block anything not an emergency from stealing your time. Below is a sample daily schedule. You can create your own following this guide.

My Schedule for _____ (Date)

Time of the Day	Activity
5:45 a.m. to 6:10 a.m.	Read my "success" book.
6:10 a.m. to 6:15 a.m.	Review my goals for the day.
6:15 a.m. to 7:00 a.m.	Get ready for school. Eat breakfast.
7:00 a.m. to 7:30 a.m.	Travel to school. Listen to inspirational audiobook.
7:30 a.m. to 3:15 p.m.	School. Use breaks and lunch to get ahead of work.
3:15 p.m. to 3:45 p.m.	Travel home. Listen to inspirational audiobook.
3:45 p.m. to 4:00 p.m.	Eat snack at home. Read "success" book while eating.
4:00 p.m. to 5:00 p.m.	Time to practice my passion activity or hobby.
5:00 p.m. to 5:30 p.m.	Bathe and get ready for dinner.
5:30 p.m. to 6:00 p.m.	Dinner.
6:00 p.m. to 7:30 p.m.	Homework/Study
7:30 p.m. to 8:00 p.m.	Contact my academic friends & discuss challenges

8:00 p.m. to 8:30 p.m.	Review and work on clarifying my goals.
8:30 p.m. to 9:00 p.m.	Eat a snack and get ready for bed.
9:00 p.m. to 9:30 p.m.	Read my "success" book.
9:30 p.m. to 5:45 a.m.	Sleep.

You may be thinking right now, *I can't do this. This is too much.* One of the hardest things I had to do as a teen was overcome my self-limiting beliefs. I had to stop saying, "Oh that's for white people, not for Mexicans (Blacks, etc.)." Let me tell you that these, time management strategies don't care what your background or heritage is. Most of you are under achieving. And to prove that you too are capable of organizing your time, I want you to imagine there's a million dollars at stake. Think of this as a 30-day million-dollar challenge where you'll have a time management expert following you around, logging down on their clipboard everything you do. After the 30 days are up, if you prioritized your actions and created daily schedules, the million dollars are yours. How likely are you to change your disorganized ways now? Would you,

1) Give up spending time with the *homies* across the street or at the skate park?
2) Stop texting boys or girls all day long?
3) Get off Snapchat, Instagram, YouTube, and all social media?
4) Stop over-sleeping?
5) Keep your room clean and tidy?
6) Stop talking excessively in class when you're supposed to be working?

7) Give up the game console gaming apps?
8) Not commit to being in a serious relationship until you can master your time?

The million dollars will be yours. Not today, but I guarantee you that if you follow my advice you will one day be a millionaire.

Being great at time management takes lots of practice. You have to build up the habit like a muscle. You have to pretend you're already great at it so you act the part of a highly effective machine. You have to model yourself after a person you know who is already great at time management. Be like them. You have to get so good at it, that you can teach other kids your age how to be expert time managers. In fact, start a blog on Google Blogger and document your journey. Invite your acquaintances at school to "subscribe" to your blog in return for ten tips on time management. I'm getting ahead of myself here.

As students of color, you have it harder than the white kids at your school. You don't have access to the privileges the white kids enjoy because they're white. There are stereotypes white adults have of you deep in their minds that you have to disprove. So you have to work twice as hard to earn and make everything you desire happen. That's just the way it is and it isn't changing. So put on your big boy or big girl *chonies* and do more with the time you have. Twice more!

Chapter 10 Main Points:

1. Squeeze out as much time out of your day as you possibly can by eliminating time wasteful activities.
2. Two time management strategies you should be utilizing are prioritizing your activities for each day and creating a daily schedule.
3. Motivate yourself to follow time management strategies by pretending that $1 million dollars are at stake and will be yours if you stay on schedule daily for at least a month.
4. As students of color, you have to work twice as hard, with the same amount of time, as white students to make your goals and dreams come true. It's not fair, but so what. Life isn't fair.

Chapter 11
Stop Reading The 3 F's: Fantasies, Fairytales, and Fiction

I enjoyed reading fiction for a very long time. From the time I came to America in 1983 to about the time I started investing in the stock market in 2005, most of the material I read was fiction. Short stories and novels were my favorite. I admired the talent of great authors like Steinbeck, Orwell, Vonnegut, and Faulkner. So much so that I wanted to be a fiction author myself. One problem, English was my second language. This meant that I had to get really good at writing a language that was foreign to me.

My dream of becoming a fiction writer began during junior college. With no formal coaching or writing training, I wrote a few short stories. They were bad. I didn't even want to share them with anyone. I put them away in a drawer at home and moved on with my collegiate studies. At UC Santa Barbara I wrote a few more short stories during my spare time. I got the nerve to share them with my roommates and friends. They humored me and said the stories were good. I entered the stories in writing contests and…I lost. I submitted story after story into contests until I got to be around 30 years of age. I kept getting rejected for publication and I didn't know why.

I took a break from writing short stories to study the craft some more, buying *non*-fiction books that covered all of the elements, for example, plot, theme, and point of view. Your English teacher has probably taught you how each of these elements of fiction work together in a story. Some students go to college and major in English, specializing in creative writing. These students know for a fact they want to write stories for a living.

I on the other hand, majored in science and knew I wanted to be a science teacher. Becoming a fiction author was something I could do on the side. I'd have a stable job as a teacher, and in my spare time, write as often as possible. The non-fiction books on creative writing, as well as online articles written by published authors to help beginners, was how I educated myself and caught up to college graduates with English degrees.

My perseverance once again paid off. I had my first short story, *The Curb*, published online in 2011. I had three other short stories, *Challenger, Los Malandros,* and *The Freight Train*, published within two years. I then put a collection of my short stories together and self-published them in 2013 as an eBook: *Immigrant Me & Other Short Stories.* Over 400 copies of the book have been downloaded at Amazon to this date. That's not very many. Why so few? I did a poor job of marketing the book.

In Chapter 4, I taught you that writing and taking Profitable Action on a Big SMART goal leads you to uncharted territory. You'll find yourself facing new problems that you must figure out how to solve as you go. I had no idea how to market my own book so once again I turned to the Internet and non-fiction books. I've spent the past three years learning all about the book publishing industry.

Non-fiction books is where the money is at

If you're wondering why I shared the previous story with you, it's so you realize that there is a purpose in everything. What is your purpose for reading fiction books about wizards, fantasy worlds, and supernatural beings? Are you looking to one day become an author of these genres? More than likely you read these types of books because your friends recommend them or you want put your imagination to the test. This is commendable. After all, it is better to read something than nothing at all.

However, if you want to accelerate your journey to the land of success, I want you to stop reading fiction. The only fiction you should be reading is what you're assigned to read by your Language Arts teachers. Your English teachers will hate me for this, but they have little experience becoming successful outside of the education industry. They believe it's critical for you to learn how to analyze a story. That's why they have you highlight, write little notes and stick them on a bunch of pages, and find evidence of the author's message in passages. I'm not going to tell you this is a useless skill. Critical reading is an extremely important skill to have, but you must also learn how to analyze non-fiction writing.

Being successful in some general education classes in college, for example, English and History, will depend on your ability to analyze text. Unfortunately, this skill isn't used in many other college courses. You won't need it if you're a science, math, engineering, business, accounting, psychology, sociology, anthropology, or finance major. The content students read in these courses is primarily non-fiction.

Reading mostly fiction at school or home is a big reason why many high school seniors do poorly on their college readiness test. They've simply not been exposed enough to non-fiction texts. Luckily, a big change is coming. One thing that is good about the Common Core Standards, you may have heard of these, is that they require English and Language Arts teachers to assign more non-fiction reading.

You can't wait for teachers to get their act together. You need to put down those fantasy tales and read non-fiction books (like this one) effective immediately. I imagine this can be tough to start doing without guidance. That's why I'm going to recommend exactly what your non-fiction focus should be.

First, start by reading non-fiction books on the things you love to do. Do you love to play video games? I recommend you read a book like, *Video Game Programming for Kids,* by Jonathan S. Harbour. You wish you could skateboard all day? Well, you can't. But you can read a book like, *Tony Hawk: Professional Skateboarder*, by Tony Hawk and Sean Mortimer. Do you get excited when other girls let you style their hair? Pick up a copy of *How to Startup & Manage Your Own Hair Salon: And Make It BIG In The Salon Business,* by Linda L. Chappo. Are you an athlete? Then you must read *Coach Wooden's Pyramid of Success,* by John Wooden and Jay Carty.

Reading non-fiction books on your hobbies and interests has an additional benefit. If you focus enough on a singular topic, reading over a hundred books, you will become an expert or authority on the subject. You will have the material to start a business coaching others, being a consultant, doing live seminars, and authoring books you can sell especially if you become an authority in an area people need help with. There is more money to be made than you can imagine. If you don't have an interest or hobby, below are topics you can read about that people are always looking for help with. The key is to focus your reading efforts on just one, once you decide which one interests you the most:

1. Motivation
2. Leadership
3. Personal Success
4. Habits
5. Fear of Failure
6. Anxiety
7. Depression
8. Relationships
9. Change
10. Self-Esteem
11. Public Speaking

Becoming an expert or authority in any one of the above topics doesn't require a college education. It requires time, which you have a lot more of as young people, a library card, and an urgency to read and keep reading.

Read non-fiction books on personal finance and money

In Chapter 9, I agreed with how most of you feel about school: schools do suck. I'm going to share with you yet another reason why most schools in America suck. Most schools in this country suck because they aren't teaching you anything about money and personal finance.

What is personal finance? Personal finance involves the knowledge of properly managing money and making the best financial decisions for you or your future family.

We are just recovering from one of the worst financial disasters in American history. Thousands of people lost their jobs and homes during the Great Recession that began in 2007. Indeed, I had many students who moved away, moved in with other family, and who were even homeless. I won't write about the causes of the Great Recession or who was to blame for it. That doesn't help in any way at this point. I will share with you why and how many people, perhaps even your own parents or extended family, were hurt by it.
Several years before the Great Recession the government made it easy for people to buy houses. There was very little regulation in the banking industry, meaning there were few laws that kept banks from doing shady things. Today you need a great credit score, a 20% down payment, and proof of sufficient income and little debt to even be considered for a home loan. Not back then. Almost anyone could get a home loan with little to no money down, bad credit, and without solid proof of sufficient monthly income. Of course the loans banks were giving these type of borrowers, the least actually able to afford a mortgage (the home loan), were garbage. These bad loans were called, sub-prime.
The majority of sub-prime loans were the type that adjusted in 2-5 years. The interest rates (you have to pay banks an interest payment on any loan) were low at the beginning, anywhere from 2 to 4%.

This was the hook that fooled a bunch of people. They couldn't resist owning a house at such a small monthly payment. But then after the 2-5 years were up, the interest rates on those loans went up (to between 6 and 9%) and the payments became unaffordable. People stopped making their monthly house payments and their homes went into a process called, foreclosure. After a few months of being delinquent on their payments, people either moved out or they were evicted from their homes.

How did so many people fall into this financial death spiral? First, people followed the crowd. Following the crowd means to do what everyone else is doing. You know how the word spreads at school about something cool and then everyone else wants a piece of the action? The same thing happens to adults who don't want to be the only one in the neighborhood not doing something everyone else is doing.

Second, people relied on the experts to explain how the home buying process worked. Regular people went to deal happy real estate agents for information. These real estate agents then convinced almost everyone into purchasing a home using these easily available sub-prime loans. I want to be clear that I'm not blaming real estate agents; they were doing what anyone else would've done, take advantage of the situation.

Lastly, people were signing contracts and home loan documents they didn't even understand. Most people weren't even reading what was written in these documents. This is what I want you to remember the most about this section: without a solid financial education, you will be taken advantage of and you'll make serious money mistakes. Making mistakes is how you learn, but some mistakes are worth avoiding.

At my blog, www.commoncoremoney.com, I often write articles for teens and young adults that teach financial concepts and money mastery. I know that very few schools in America offer financial literacy classes, and this is a great tragedy. The Great Recession could've been less severe if more adults had learned simple financial skills like budgeting, saving for emergencies, saving for retirement, and how credit, loans, and interest work.

It's still not too late for you. You can't expect your parents to sit you down one day and transfer what they know about money to you. They may not know much! You can't expect your teachers to get you up to speed on being financially literate. Most of them are clueless about finances. Half of them can't tell you the difference between a stock and a bond. So once again, you have to take the initiative and teach yourself.

I taught myself everything I know about money, personal finance, business, and investing. How did I do this? You guessed it. I read over 100 books on these topics over the course of five years. They helped me become a millionaire and secure my retirement. I firmly believe they can help you be rich one day too. So let me recommend and strongly suggest you read these additional non-fiction book or article topics before you enroll at a university:

1. Personal Finance
2. Personal and Family Budgets
3. Credit Cards
4. Home Mortgages
5. Student College Loans
6. Car Loans

7. Investing General
8. Investing in Stocks
9. Investing in Real Estate
10. Retirement Saving Vehicles
11. Checking, Savings, and Brokerage Bank Accounts
12. Taxes, Personal
13. Taxes, Business
14. Insurance

It's okay if you don't get to all of them before college. If you become a lifelong learner like I am, you'll be reading until you grow old. But if I were you, I'd make reading about personal finance a priority. The last thing you want is to be a statistic in the next Great Recession. You want to be able to see the next financial crisis coming and be in a situation where you can capitalize (make money) on it.

Chapter 11 Main Points:

1. You should only be reading the three f's (fantasies, fairytales, and fiction) if you plan on one day being a fiction author.
2. Reading non-fiction books or articles will pay off the most for your future.
3. Focusing your reading activity on one non-fiction area of interest will set-you up to be an authority figure, commanding big fees for coaching others, helping businesses as a consultant, or for speaking engagements. As an expert in a field, you can also write and sell multiple books.
4. Investing in your financial education will pay you back tenfold. Being financially literate is

the only way you can avoid making bad money decisions.

Chapter 12

Skip Going To A Four-Year University After High School

One of the smartest financial decisions I ever made as a teen was enrolling at San Jose City College in the summer of 1994. I was a 17-year-old, fresh out of high school, when I took my first college class, pre-Calculus. I had been accepted to several universities during my senior year, but I decided not to attend any one of them. You may think that my decision to stay home and attend a junior college instead of a four-year university had to do with money. It actually had to do with my lack of maturity.

I was a total momma's boy growing up. My Mexican mother did just about everything for me. She did my laundry, cooked my breakfast and dinner, made my bed, ironed my pants, and even served me my plate at the kitchen table. Some days she'd even wake me up for school! Even though I was very independent outside of my home, I was still dependent on my mother at home. Anytime I visited the homes of friends that happened to be Mexican like me, their mothers were the same as mine, traditional. This was not good at all.

It may have been nice and convenient at the time to have my mother do the things I should've been doing for myself, but it had the effect of making me unable to fend for myself. I couldn't go off to a four-year college and live in a dorm. I didn't even know how to wash clothes! The only thing I knew how to "cook" was Top Ramen noodles and a bowl of cereal. Going to a 2-year college first was necessary for me. It bought me the time I needed to learn everyday life skills.

I'm not going to lie. Going to a 2-year college after high school was like coming in second place. Many of my friends went straight to a four-year university, including my buddy, Malik. I felt left out. Making things worse was the attitude the top students in my senior class had about junior college. It was a joke to rename the local junior colleges after big time universities. For example, De Anza College on Stevens Creek Boulevard was dubbed, U.S.C, or University of Stevens Creek. Seniors who were going to enroll at De Anza College saved face by mockingly calling it U.S.C., after the famous University of Southern California. Go Trojans!

De Anza College was and still is an excellent place to learn after high school, yet back then many high school students considered themselves losers if they had to start out at a 2-year college. Oh how wrong they were. Even back in the mid to late '90s, four-year universities were expensive to attend. Meanwhile, the units and books at a 2-year college were a whole lot cheaper. What I enjoyed the most of my time at San Jose City College, however, was being able to take classes with older adults as my classmates.

I spent two years at SJCC, and because I was on the track team, I had to register for many evening courses. These classes were always small, no more than 20 to 25 students, and the professors were very personable. As an 18 and 19-year-old, I was interacting with grown-ups with jobs. On breaks, they would share with me what they did for work, stories about their kids, and why they were furthering their education. I was getting an excellent education about the real world unintentionally. But more importantly, I was saving a lot of money doing it.

You should only go to a four-year college after high school if...

Unless you're getting a full or partial scholarship, don't be a sucker and enroll in a four-year college after high school. Universities have taken advantage of a loophole provided to them by the government. This scheme has allowed universities to increase their fees for years without any penalty. The racket is this: the government makes it easy for all high school graduates with college acceptance letters to get federal student loans. University officials know that they can increase their tuition fees and students will still pay because 1) most students will not get denied a loan and 2) the need for a college degree is not diminishing.

There is not much that can stop universities from raising their prices. Every year, there is a fresh batch of high school seniors all over America applying to several universities to increase their odds of "getting in" somewhere. This situation has made many adults angry at the people who run colleges and universities. How can they take advantage of these poor young men and women? Why do they treat these college kids like numbers? These are the questions being asked today by concerned politicians, educators, the public, and many others. But the answer is obvious: colleges are businesses and making as much money as they can keeps them open.

Many college graduates are very sorry they even went to college. Why? Because after graduation they have student loan debt that is as much as what some houses are selling for. The average yearly cost of attending a public, in-state university was $25K to $28K during the 2015-16 school year. With financial aid and grants, the average amount of debt a student will owe by the time they graduate is between $20K and $30K. It doesn't seem like that much, does it? But...

Because many college students don't major in something that will lead to a job right out of college, they apply to graduate school. Graduate school is college for college graduates. This is where students work on a professional or career program and earn either a Masters or a Ph.D. degree. For example, if you want to be a physical therapist, the route many students take starts first with a major in Kinesiology. Kinesiology is the study of body movements. Then every student that graduates with a Kinesiology degree must apply to a Physical Therapy (P.T.) program if being a physical therapist is their career goal.

The price tag for going to any graduate school program is higher than undergraduate studies, and the financial aid is even harder to get. This means that students that get into P.T., Pharmacist, Medical, Law, Education, Dental, graduate school programs have to pay for their schooling with more loans. Loans they have to start repaying exactly six months after they graduate from their program. Finding a job quickly after graduate school so you can start making money and paying off student loans will be your number one priority if studying for a career is your goal.

I have many younger professional friends who left graduate school owing more than $100K in student loans. Some have started their careers and are being paid so low that they can barely afford to pay their loan payments and rent a place to live in. Many college graduates move back in with their parents to save money. It's a sensible idea if you don't mind living again with your parents and following their house rules. Some young adults find it hard to give up all the freedom they had while attending college and they don't enjoy moving back in with their folks. But it's a choice they must commit to, whether they like it or not, if they're ever to fully payoff their student loans and get out of debt.

The most nightmarish cases I have come across have been published online for all of America to read. These are the sad stories of college graduates who made terrible decisions while attending college, using credit cards given to them on campus without understanding how credit cards work, and racking up huge sums of debt. These are also the sad stories of young people who went to college, got out, and couldn't find a job because their college degree was practically worthless. Many of them gave up and got jobs as bartenders or restaurant servers. Finally, there are also many unfortunate stories of college students who decided more than halfway through that college wasn't for them, dropping out. They wasted both their time and money.

Know this: as of today, college student loans can't be forgiven, and a person can't file for bankruptcy to get out of having to pay for their loans.

What is bankruptcy? Bankruptcy is a process that allows individuals or businesses to file for an "automatic stay" in federal court. The automatic stay keeps creditors from taking any action to collect the money owed by these individuals or businesses. Basically, people who file for bankruptcy admit to the judge that they are broke, and can't pay the people they owe money to. Getting your creditors off your back may sound like a great deal, except that the process also happens to ruin your credit for seven years. With bad credit, you can't buy a car, a house, or even get a credit card.

You're on the hook for every dollar you borrowed while going to college. If you borrowed from private college loan lenders, and you stop making your payments, good luck getting them to stop bothering you. They will call, mail, and email to make sure you pay what you owe them. They will treat you very poorly and have collectors call you nonstop. Does any of this sound fun?

If what I wrote above about college scared you, then you need to toughen up. I need you to know the truth about college. Going to college is one of the most important financial decisions you'll ever make and you should make it with as much knowledge at your disposal as possible. The good news is that the financial impact of your decision to attend college can be lessened.

Start at a 2-year college then transfer to your four-year college of choice

Again, unless you're being offered a full or partial scholarship, there is no need to start at a four-year college. Every college freshman and sophomore must take general education courses (pre-requisites) before gaining access to classes relating to their major. Even though I wanted to major in Biology, I still had to take classes like English, Political Science, and History. Doing these pre-requisite courses at San Jose City College saved me thousands of dollars over two years. I lived with my parents, saving money on "room and board," and ate my parent's food. The meal plans offered at a university are quite expensive.

An additional benefit of going to a two-year college first is that you won't get sucked into the college life culture. Universities these days are more like country clubs. They provide students with pools, enormous gyms and playing fields, and social gathering venues. Every student enjoys these amenities, until they realize that they're the ones paying for them. There is a lot more peer pressure in college too. A university is like its own little city where the majority of the population is teenagers and people in their early twenties. Crazy things can happen when a bunch of young people are together with few adult role models.

If you qualify for financial aid you can also get it at a Junior college. The financial aid I received at SJCC paid for my tuition and more. I worked only two days a week, Saturday and Sunday, and still had more than enough to pay all of my Junior college expenses and save for a car. Transportation to and from the college campus is not a problem if you live in the dorms, but once you're forced to move out and give up your dorm room to a new freshman, you'll need either a used car or a monthly bus pass. The $800 used Camaro I bought worked reliably for about a year and a half, getting me from my home in central San Jose to the SJCC campus in northwest San Jose. But then the transmission on the car stopped working and I couldn't afford fixing it or buying another car. I had to transfer to UC Santa Barbara without a vehicle of my own to drive around. My solution was buying a bicycle to get around.

The places available to rent near campus will be the most expensive. Landlords know students want to be as close as possible to campus, so they list rooms, apartments, and homes for rent higher than what these same places would rent for in the city or town. If you don't mind using public transportation, you can save between $100 and $200 on rent every month living a few miles away from the university. I had to take the transit bus to get to and from SJCC. I spent about 35 minutes on the bus (one-way) and I used the time wisely. I'd read from my textbooks or from books I checked out from the school library. It was some of my most productive time.

The three most important things you have to keep in mind when attending a 2-year college are, 1) Your pace, 2) Your persistence, and 3) The transferability of your courses. Many educators discourage their students to attend a 2-year college because they know the odds are against these same students finishing their 2-year associate degree and successfully transferring to a 4-year college.

A January 2016 report by Community College Research Center's Davis Jenkins and John Fink stated that only about 42% of all community college students that transfer to a four-year college earn a bachelor's degree within six years of starting their higher education studies. The rate is worse for low-income students. Only about 36% of poor students who transfer to a four-year college complete their bachelor's degree within six years of starting college. You may be asking, what about those that didn't transfer to a four-year college? Sadly, only about

14% of all students who enroll at a junior college will transfer to a four-year college, and earn a bachelors degree within six years of starting out.

Why do so few students transfer and complete their bachelor's degree in six years or less? Once again it comes down to your preparation. If you didn't prepare well for college level classes, you will do poorly on the placement exams after high school. This means that you will have more remedial courses to take. Getting stuck having to take remedial classes discourages average people. They don't have the perseverance to keep going, no matter how long it takes. Once they get tired emotionally, they give up and drop out. You can't be this type of person. You can't quit!

If you have the preparation and persistence to handle college level classes, you can't delay while attending junior college. You have to take a full class load. For junior colleges on semester tracks, this means you take five classes at a time. This is how I was able to graduate with my associate degree in two years and transfer to UCSB. I took five classes a semester for two straight years. I didn't work full time. My job was studying daily, doing my assignments, and going to track and field practice. (I ran for the SJCC track team).

If you have to take five remedial classes, this means just one more semester, not two or three more. Only uncommitted people stretch out their junior college education by taking the minimal number of classes to be considered a "full-time" student; usually this is four total classes a semester. However, if you're working several days a week, especially to save money for future college expenses, taking four classes a semester instead of five is a good idea. You don't want to "burn out."

If getting a bachelor's degree at a four-year college is your goal, then you must be on alert every time you register for classes while attending junior college. Many junior college students transfer to a state college. Transferring to a more prestigious public university or a private school is totally different. Each type of university has their own transfer requirements, and the classes offered at a junior college must be "transferable" to the university you will be transferring to.

For example, I didn't want to transfer to San Jose State or any of the state colleges in California. I wanted to attend a university that was part of the "UC" system. The classes I took at SJCC all had to be transferable to UC schools, otherwise, I was wasting my time and money taking them. There are counselors you can talk to in the counseling office of each junior college to make sure the classes you select are transferable to the university you plan on applying to.

Successful people are proactive. They are the first ones to get in line, make appointments, fill-out and turn-in necessary forms, and ask questions. You must embrace being proactive once you start attending college because unlike high school, there won't be any office passes for you being delivered to your classes. No one will check in on you academically. Attending a two-year college will allow you to get a good idea of the type of proactivity you'll need to be successful at a four-year college. It's a whole lot easier to get lost in the system at a large university. This is why cultivating a habit of being proactive while at junior college will make your life as a transfer student that much smoother.

Chapter 12 Main Points:

1. Going to a junior college after high school doesn't mean you've failed. On the contrary, today it's an incredibly smart decision.
2. Going to a junior college buys you time to mature and learn the necessary everyday life skills you'll need to survive on your own (without your mom).
3. Four-year colleges and universities are business entities. They operate to make a profit, not necessarily to give you the best value for your dollars.
4. Going to a two-year college first will reduce the amount of college loans you'll need to complete your bachelor's degree.
5. Have the persistence and dedication to complete your two-year college associate degree as quickly as possible, no matter how many remedial classes you need to take.
6. Be proactive from day one. It's up to you to make sure you're enrolling in the right classes, completing the necessary coursework to be accepted to the university of your choice as a transfer student.

Chapter 13
You're Born A Lamborghini, But Live Like A Bucket

The Lamborghini is my favorite car. Stunning from every angle, these cars seem unreal. They don't belong on earth; they belong in outer space with the stars. Every human on this planet is born a Lamborghini, unique and beautiful. The master designer, evolution, has worked on you for thousands of years and your organs, muscles, and skeleton have made you capable of ruling an entire planet. And this is why I have a hard time understanding people who treat their body like an old, run-down bucket car.

Did you know that staying fit and healthy is a top five New Year's resolution almost every year? Most adults have the hardest time staying fit, losing weight, and being healthy. That's why they make getting in shape a top priority to start every year. They do this by going out and buying a gym membership. Some even pay for a trainer. They exercise consistently for about a month and a half, and then they stop. They never had the habit of exercising fully developed within them, so they go back to their old ways, rarely exercising and eating poorly.

I dislike going to the gym in January. It's the most crowded time of the year. The New Year's resolution crowd rolls in so that by the second week of January, it's hard to get my workout done in an hour, my usual length of time. But by mid-February, the last of the New Year's resolution crowd is staying home, avoiding the gym, and I get my gym back. It's estimated that only around 20% of the people who sign up for a gym membership in January stay past February.

Successful people eat and rest well. They exercise daily and understand the connection between how they treat their body, and how their body treats them. They know that people are living longer and they want to be one of those people. Why? They have a great life, and they want to keep living it as long as possible. You see, you can have all the money in the world, but you can't buy eternal life. If you become wealthy or successful at the expense of your health, you won't be around long enough to enjoy what you've built.

It's true: You are what you eat

Do you know what the food pyramid is? I'm sure you have seen an image of the food pyramid somewhere; if not in a classroom, then for sure in the nurse's office at school. The food pyramid explains nutrition in an easy to understand fashion. It shows you what you should be eating daily and how many portions of these types of foods to eat so that you have a balanced diet. Unfortunately, few people follow the advice of the food pyramid and instead eat a diet high in fat, salt, and sugar. It's no wonder why America has one of the highest rates of obesity in the country.

Everywhere you go, you have to eat like you're a Lamborghini. If you respect yourself, you will eat junk food in moderation and not make it your entire daily diet. If you owned a Lamborghini, and loved your car, would you fuel it up with the cheap gasoline at the gas station? Every high end, luxury sports car requires premium gasoline, the most expensive type. If you fill up the tank of a Lamborghini with low grade, unleaded gasoline, you'll hear something called a spark knock. This is a high-pitched pinging and rattling noise. If you keep this up, the spark knock can cause long-term damage.

Our own bodies don't produce such an obvious noise when we consume too much of the wrong types of foods. Sure you can get a bellyache if you overeat, and even feel bad temporarily. But your body, unlike a car, is an adaptable machine. You have the ability to store fat, and to get addicted to sugar. So once you go down the road of overeating daily, it becomes harder for you to turn back. If you eat foods rich in fat and sugar, you can become obese and worse, possibly diabetic, especially if you don't exercise regularly.

As an educator, I see students eating nutritious foods (baby carrots, celery sticks, pretzels, apples, trail mix, etc.) and I also see students eating junk food ("hot" potato chips, cookies, candies, breakfast pastries, etc.) as snacks. The same goes for what students drink daily at school. Some bring water bottles while others bring sports drinks and sodas. Sadly, sometimes parents contribute to the problem by buying fast food and delivering it to the school for their child to eat during lunch.

The food available in school cafeterias has improved over the years, and the meals these days must meet federal regulations. This is great because now students have the option to eat better food at school. However, there are still places on a school campus where students can buy sweets or soft drinks. I believe in giving students the choice to make the right decision and am not in favor of banning certain types of food from schools, but the reality of the situation is that most of you lack self-control. You're okay with treating your body like a bucket instead of a Lamborghini, even when you know better.

Successful people stay active and know that staying healthy is their responsibility. They understand that exercising has the power to clear their mind and boost their mood. When your mind is clear and your mood is boosted, you can accomplish more at school. If you happen to play basketball, football, or soccer on the blacktop during lunch, you may have noticed how much calmer and focused you are once you return to class. Some of you have a hard time sitting still and paying attention, but once you get a chance to exercise either in P.E. or at lunch, you do better in your later periods.

Many of you believe P.E. is a class that's meant to force you to exercise. Not so. P.E. is a class designed to teach you the fundamentals of athletic movement, and to build the habit of exercising in you by forcing you into a routine. To get an "A" in P.E. you have to dress out daily, and participate in all the activities as directed by the P.E. teacher. Many of you earn a bad grade in P.E. because you decide not to dress out some days. You'd rather not sweat and get stinky because your social status at school is more important. You don't get that your social status at school will last but a few years, yet your failure to create the habit of exercise will impact you for the rest of your life.

Pretend you have an athletic competition tomorrow

I started to really watch what I was eating in high school when I decided to compete in track and field. The school lunches were horrible in my era. Pizza, nachos, corn dog, hamburger, and cup of noodles, were some of the foods the cafeteria served each school week. My coach would lecture us on not eating these types of food because they would affect our workouts at practice. At first I didn't believe him, but then I noticed that every time I ate the school lunch, I'd throw up during hard workouts.

I wanted to be the best at track practice. I didn't want any teammate taking my spot on the mile-relay team. That competitive fire made me alter my diet. Instead of eating the free school lunch, I asked my mom to cook me pasta, rice, baked chicken, potatoes, and fish. These were some of the meals I had Monday through Friday at school:

1) Spaghetti with lean ground beef
2) Baked chicken with steam rice
3) Baked potato with some cheddar cheese and baked chicken
4) Oven roasted potatoes and fish
5) Chicken salad with a little bit of Thousand Island dressing
6) Tuna sandwich

How can you transform your weekly diet to include healthier versions of the foods you love to eat? Be creative!

My mom wanted to know why I couldn't just eat the Mexican food she cooked for dinner. I broke it to her gently: "My coach says Mexican food has too much *manteca* (lard)." I had to stop her the next day from going down to the school to talk to my coach. Even though my mom was mad at first, eventually she too came around to the advice of my coach and started using olive oil to cook her meals. The whole family benefited.

It's hard to change your diet without some sort of motivation. I wanted to the best athlete I could be, and always perform at my peak. You may not be an athlete, but you may enjoy doing other types of physical activity regularly like riding a bike, skateboarding, dancing, surfing, or hiking. Consider eating like an athlete to be the best at your activity. In fact, even if you aren't active, I want you to pretend you're an athlete and you have a competition the following day. From Monday through Saturday, eat like the Olympics are tomorrow and you're in them. You want that gold medal and the only way you're getting it is if you have the right fuel to give your body the edge over your competition.

Pretend the Olympics are over on Sunday. This is your cheat day. On Sunday, you can the foods you craved for all week. You don't get to pig out. You simply get to eat the things you like when it's time to have breakfast, lunch, dinner, and snacks in between. Your cheat day is a reward for respecting your body the other six days of the week. It's very difficult to stay motivated to eat well without indulging yourself once in a while.

One final tip: drink plenty of water every day. Did you know you're supposed to be drinking at least 2-liters (half a gallon) of water a day? Drinking water has great health benefits. Water will,

1. Make you feel less tired.
2. Boost your mood.
3. Help relieve headaches.
4. Help with digestion and constipation.

5. Flush out bad chemicals from your body.
6. Fool you into thinking you're full so you eat less.

I am seeing more students carry around water at school. This is a fantastic trend that I hope keeps going.

So, are you a Lamborghini or a bucket car? The answer is: A Lamborghini! Successful people know how intricately connected great health is with their current and future success. The two go hand in hand. This is why I need you to either continue eating a healthy diet if you're already doing it, or to start eating healthy today.

Chapter 13 Main Points:

1. Successful people respect their bodies because they know that staying on top requires great health and fitness.
2. When you see yourself as a Lamborghini and an athlete that's about to compete, you'll trick your mind and eat better food, consume snacks and junk food in moderation, and drink water instead of sugary beverages.
3. Live your life like a Lamborghini, and not like a bucket car.

Chapter 14
Popularity Is More Important Now Than Ever Before

Let's be real, everyone wants to be "popular." The desire to be popular never goes away, except that in the adult world, popularity is called, "recognition." In middle school, the only way I knew how to get popular was by being bad in class. I would purposely push the teacher's buttons to get kicked out. I'd try really hard to make the pretty girls laugh by being a clown, hoping to get one of them to like me. Being a troublemaker also made me popular among the cool boys. The consequence of my behavior though was getting nothing positive out of my middle school experience. All of it was negative and the worst part was that I had to start over; the popularity race started once again in high school.

From being a teen and from working at four different high schools, I've learned how important it can be for you not to feel unpopular at school. Nobody wants to spend 3 years (middle school) or 4 years (high school) at a place where others ignore you or worse, don't even see you. I started high school the same way I left middle school using the only formula I knew to build my reputation.

Unfortunately that formula wasn't going to work in high school where the consequences were more severe. When the vice principal says your name in front of other kids and he's not happy to see you, that is never a good thing. If this is happening to you right now, congratulations, you're on the radar for a potential school expulsion.

Girls have their own unique way of building their reputation and popularity at school. Sadly, many of them do it through ways that also get lead to negative attention. Do you constantly dress to impress or wear revealing clothing? Do you find yourself in a bunch of girl drama all the time, getting into verbal or physical fights with other girls at school? Do you "talk" to boys who are in a relationship with someone else? If you answered "yes" to any of these questions, you have something in common with my younger self: low self-esteem.

Low self-esteem was the reason I sought any type of attention at school. Since the only type of attention I knew how to get was the bad kind, I went with it. It boosted my low self-esteem just the same as positive attention. Or so I thought. The problem with negative attention is that it's like eating a chocolate bar. It gives you a temporary high, but then you come crashing down and sink even further low. Positive attention is more permanent and healthy for your self-esteem. But just how do you get it?

Organic popularity versus strategic popularity

What is organic popularity? Organic popularity is popularity gained naturally, meaning, without any effort. There are teens that become popular not even trying to do so. You may be hanging out with some of them. One day they're average, and another day they blow up and everyone on campus knows who they are. Kids at school become overnight sensations by doing great things. These "great things" can include,

1. Getting on the local news for doing something positive around the community, like helping the homeless or saving abused animals.
2. Winning a state or national competition in science (science fair) or technology (robotics).
3. Getting on the local news for being a kid entrepreneur. Perhaps they started a small business whose positive reputation has spread through word of mouth.
4. Getting accepted to several Ivy League schools like Stanford, Yale, or Harvard.
5. Being a star athlete whose individual efforts have turned around a once losing program.
6. Winning the talent competition at school by singing or dancing like they belong on television.
7. Uploading a drum or guitar solo video to YouTube that gets thousands of views.

Sometimes teens aren't intending to become popular at school, but they become so nonetheless because they have an inner genius or a skill that they have developed over a long time. When this inner genius or developed skill is finally discovered, it has the effect of turning lots of heads.

Justin Bieber is a perfect example of a teen that became popular getting fans organically. He uploaded a video of himself singing and playing the piano and within days he had a strong YouTube following. He did this several times until he was discovered and the rest is history. I don't think anyone (other than himself perhaps) expected him to become such a star, but a star he became.

Sydney McLaughlin is another example of a teen whose popularity grew organically. In 2016 at the age of 16, she became one of the youngest track and field athletes to make the U.S. Olympic team and compete in the Olympics. Can you imagine all the praise and positive attention she got at her school? She may not have even wanted the attention, but she got it nonetheless.

One final example of a kid that gained her popularity organically is Mikaila Ulmer. In 2016, Mikaila scored a deal worth 11 million dollars with Whole Foods. She appeared on the hit television show, Shark Tank, where she pitched her socially conscious business, BeeSweet Lemonade, and partnered with multi-millionaire entrepreneur, Daymond John. Saving bees and beekeepers all while providing a tasty beverage. Not bad for an 11-year-old.

What is strategic popularity? Strategic popularity involves the active attempt to get popular. Kids who are willing to do what is outside of the comfort zone of most other kids are using strategic popularity methods. Here is a list of what it looks like when kids are using strategic popularity techniques at school:

1. They frequently volunteer to represent their class at a pep rally competition.
2. They join a social or "outgoing" club at school like ASB and run for office.
3. They're nice to and befriend everyone, no matter the social group the other kids belong to.
4. They're the first to get a driver's license (and car) and they offer rides home or to the local fast food restaurant to only the cool kids.

5. They convince their parents to allow them to throw a party Friday or Saturday night (alcohol or other drugs may be present) at their house for a "few" friends.
6. They convince their rich parents to throw them the biggest sweet sixteen or *quinceañera* party and invite only the "right" kids from school.

Hollywood has made a fortune making movies of ordinary teenagers (the main characters) who go to great lengths to become popular at school. Remember the movie, Twilight? Here we have the character, Bella, played by Kristen Stewart. Bella is an average girl who moves to a new and seemingly boring town. She has a few friends, nothing too exciting. How does she become an overnight sensation at school? That's right, she begins to date the mysterious Edward Cullen, played by Robert Pattinson, who just happens to be a 108-year-old vampire. Oh, and he's incredibly cute. It's the equivalent of an unpopular girl who gets popular by dating the quarterback of the varsity football team.

My favorite movie about strategic popularity is, Can't Buy Me Love. This 1987 classic is about a nerd by the name of Ronald Miller, played by actor, Patrick Dempsey. It's his senior year of high school, and Ronald wants it to be very different. He just can't do another year of hanging out with his nerd buddies, playing poker on Friday nights instead of being where all the cool kids are. So what does he do? He buys his popularity. Seeing head cheerleader, Cindy Mancini, played by actress, Amanda Peterson, in complete distress at the mall, Ronald agrees to pay $1,000 for a new suede outfit so that Cindy can replace the one she ruined (belonging to her mother) at a party. What does Ronald get in exchange?

Ronald gets to date Cindy Mancini, perhaps the most popular girl at school, for an entire month. Cindy has to pretend she's dating Ronald, a total outcast to her friends. Of course she can't just date a nerd like Ronald. It won't fool anyone. She has to change Ronald's entire look, giving him a complete makeover. Cindy even coaches him how to "talk" to the cool kids, something Ronald has no experience doing. This story has a "happy ending," but not before a whole lot of awkward suffering.

Out of organic and strategic popularity, which of the two do you think is best able to one-day help you become a successful adult? If you said, organic popularity, you'd be correct. Strategic popularity is worthless. Sure it feels great to be popular at school no matter how that popularity was achieved. But you can kiss your strategic popularity goodbye the day you graduate from high school. The good times are over. There is zero connection between being popular at school and being professionally successful as an adult. Because organic popularity is all about your hard work, dedication, and/or natural talent, you stand a far better chance of benefiting as an adult from what you accomplished in high school.

If you want organic popularity you're going to have to come out of your shell. You'll have to be courageous and show the world what you're capable of doing. Being overly introverted and shy won't help your personal brand.

Personal branding: the 21st century phenomenon

What is personal branding? You've come across many famous brands in your life. Nike, Coca-Cola, Apple, and Google, are all examples of brands. If the marketing (promotion) is done correctly, a person can make themselves or their career into a brand. Personal branding is basically the ongoing effort by a person to give off a lasting impression (to other people) of who they are and what they represent.

Kim Kardashian is a personal branding genius. I hope you don't consider her a reality television star. She's one savvy businesswoman whose name alone is worth millions of dollars.

Ever hear of Tai Lopez? You've probably seen his ads on YouTube. If you know of him, you may be aware that he gained his wealth by becoming a successful Internet entrepreneur. When you think Tai Lopez, you think Internet businesses. That's the power of a strong personal brand.

Now I'm not just throwing out names of famous people here. In fact, anyone who conducts business on the Internet with their name as the website address, for example, www.cosvaldogomez.com, is marketing their personal brand and business. Why is this important to you?

Well, do you ever intend on having an online presence? Let me let you in on something, you already do! Unfortunately, many of you aren't thinking about your online reputation as being worth money in the future. All successful people take great care of their cyber profile. Damaging it can mean the end of their success. You too should be safeguarding your online reputation as much as you do your reputation at school. If you ever do any side business online as an adult, or interview for a high paying job, the trash you publish today may come back to bite you.

Don't ever upload pictures or video of yourself doing things that are illegal, mean, dangerous, or stupid. You *will* be judged. Similarly, don't ever upload content of yourself complaining, talking badly about someone, or insulting a group of people. Every year, many adults lose their job for using their social media irresponsibly. Whether you like it or not, people are watching and won't hesitate to report you to your school administrators or if you have a job, your employer.

Let me share with you now why organic popularity is important. In the world you will soon be entering, the adult world, there is no shortage of ways people can make money online. Making lots of money depends on how far and wide your personal brand is able to reach people's smartphones. What do you call a person with a smartphone and a credit (or debit) card? Answer: today and tomorrow's consumer. In the 21st century, individual businesses and business owners compete to put themselves or their ads on your smartphone screen. They know this leads to people making purchases. You can be one of these business owners as an Internet entrepreneur.

What do Internet entrepreneurs do? They mostly run smart marketing (promotion) campaigns to get people to give up their email addresses. Have you ever clicked on a webpage and had a rectangular pop-up appear at the center of the screen asking for your name and email address? These may be annoying to you at your age, but believe me when I tell you that "capturing" emails is how many people have gotten rich in America this century. Think now…why do people who own webpages or websites want other people's emails? So they can send them emails! But not just any regular email.

Internet entrepreneurs who capture emails are known as email marketers. They send carefully crafted emails to their "list" (every email address they have), offering deals or products for sale. If the person who receives the email opens and reads it, there is a small chance they will buy whatever they're being sold. Small chance? Who cares, right? Wrong! Let's run some quick numbers.

Say you're an Internet entrepreneur (like Tai Lopez) who has a list consisting of 10,000 subscribers (people who gave you their name and email address) to your site. You decide to send an email to your list and offer them a $50 discount on a product you created, like a DVD, audiobook, or eBook on becoming a successful Internet entrepreneur. The cost of the product was originally $109.99, but for a "limited time" your followers can buy it for only $59.99.

Out of the 10,000 people who get the email, maybe 6,500 actually open the email. Out of these 6,500, only 5,000 read the entire email. Out of these 5,000, 100 of them decide to buy the product. In case you didn't notice, that Internet entrepreneur just made $5,999.0 from a single email. Not bad, huh?

I'm purposely leaving out a lot of detail about Internet entrepreneurship and online marketing. I wanted simply to expose you to one of many non-career options the Internet has made available. Here are some other types of online businesses you can research on your own time:

1. Blogging
2. Affiliate Marketing (Selling other people's products)
3. E-commerce (Online store)

Remember, all of these require a reputable personal brand, so keep your online activity professional.

If you start building your personal brand in high school by showcasing the best of you, the further along you will be on the road to professional success when you become an adult. I suggest that you try to make a meaningful connection with as many other students as possible at your school. Instead of people signing your yearbook, have them give you their contact information. Enter their name, email address, and phone number into your smart phone. This is your first network and it could come in handy. You never know when you'll need to tap into it.

Chapter 14 Main Points:
1. Low self-esteem is a reason why many kids desire to be popular at school. Getting negative attention to become popular damages your self-esteem in the long run.
2. When you let your inner genius or developed talents shine, you won't have to work to become popular. Popularity will come to you.
3. Strategic popularity is both useless and worthless. There is no connection between success and popularity at school, but with organic popularity, you at least have a chance of setting a foundation for your personal brand.
4. Successful people protect their online profile because they know that any negative attention could lead to the end of their success.
5. The Internet has opened the door to multiple types of online business. There has never been a better time to be an entrepreneur. A strong personal brand is the foundation to success as an Internet entrepreneur.

Chapter 15
180 Your Worst Performances Every Time

I've had many bad days in my life. Sharing the details of all of these bad days is not possible in this book. What *is* possible is telling you that your worst days and performances don't have to define you. What I've learned over the course of my life is that you can't avoid bad days; they happen. You will be great at what you do on most days, but you'll also have days where you just plain sucked.

Despite your best efforts, you'll let yourself or others down. Failing to try won't be the reason why you falter. It simply isn't possible to be at 360 degrees, to come full circle at your best, every day. Consistency has been one of the reasons for my personal success. I get up early in the morning, at least two and a half hours before I have to be at work, and I write or I read. I put in 100% at work, giving everything I have to my students, then I'm off to the gym. I get my workout in and then get home to my family. I'm a father and husband as soon as I set foot in door. I go to bed early, and I repeat my routine the next day.

The only change to my routine is on the weekends. On Saturdays and Sundays, I'm able to squeeze in more time to work on my personal brand, embracing the 21ˢᵗ century. I could easily let my foot off the accelerator, but I choose not to. Going all out like this, however, sometimes results in my having a stinker of a day. But my capacity to "let go" of the past, something I learned how to do, fuels my desire to get back on track even more energized. Having a short memory of my worst performances has allowed me to have some of my best days in my life.

The art of 180

Knowing a little geometry goes a long way. Before getting into the art of 180, you need to understand that a semi-circle has 180 degrees. Between 0 and 90 degrees you have what are known as "acute" angles. At 90 degrees, you have what's known as a "right" angle. Any angle greater than 90, but less than 180 is known as an "obtuse" angle.

Now, if you should ever have a zero degree type of day, as in awful, I want you to get in the habit of badly and desperately wanting to 180-it. What does "180-it" mean? To 180-it, you completely flip your previous poor performance. In other words, you go from worst performance to a great performance. It's not easy to go from a really bad day to a day like you've never had before. You have to intentionally forget about your mistakes and almost pretend like the awful day never happened. How do you do this? Like anything else, it's a process.

So You Had A Bad Day Exercise:

You just had an "epic fail" type of day. You were at school or at an event and your performance was out of the ordinary. Your closest friends or teammates are not faulting you because they know everyone has bad days, and what you did could easily happen to them. You're your biggest critic immediately afterward and are giving yourself hell in your head, wishing you could've done something different to change the way things went. Sound familiar?

The moments between this bad day and your next best day are the most critical, and will either make you an incredible performer or an average one. To survive these difficult hours, you need a bunch of distractions, to repeat positive affirmations, and a punching bag (pillows or cushions work just as well). Figuring out the activities that distract you the most are up to you. These could be playing video games, watching YouTube videos, or a movie at home. Stay off your social media. Other peers may be talking about you and you don't need reminders of what's already in the past.

Start your first distraction while at home. If your mind should stray from the focus of the distraction back to a mental replay of your previous lows, immediately say to yourself out-loud: "I'm great, I'll always be great, and if for some reason I'm not great on any given day, I'll be my great self once again the next day." This affirmation is meant to confirm that overall you are a top performer, but like all top performers, it isn't in your character to focus energy unnecessarily on the past. You will be very emotional after a "bad day." No doubt you'll be overly frustrated. This is where the punching bag (or pillows) comes into play. Right after saying your affirmation, release any pent up anger by punching on the bag, pillows, or cushions. Repeat this exercise as needed until you go to bed.

The fact is every top performer has a unique way of getting back in stride after a suboptimal performance and so should you. Sometimes top performers have epic performances after a really bad day. Consider the type of game NBA All-Star Stephen Curry had on November 4th, 2016. He'd made a three-point basket in 157 straight games. But on the evening he and the Golden State Warriors faced off against the Los Angeles Lakers on November 4th, his streak would come to an end. He made 10, three point shot attempts, but none of them went through the hoop.

Now you may think that a competitive athlete of such caliber like Stephen Curry would be completely upset about his horrible shooting performance immediately after the game. This is what he told the media in the locker room:

"That was a cool little ride. Would have loved to finish my career making one every game, but hey, start a new one. What was it, like two years? Kind of weird not to make one, but I will keep shooting."

Does this sound like a person who is going to leave that arena and beat himself up emotionally for his missed shots and opportunities? No! This sounds like a professional who understands that bad shooting nights will happen. This was perhaps one of his worst days on the floor in his entire NBA career, yet he's congratulating himself on all that he accomplished prior to that game against the Lakers. What's more, he's even laid out what he intends to do his next game: keep shooting and start a new streak!

And that's exactly what he did. The following game against the New Orleans Pelicans, Curry sank

13 shots from three point range, breaking the NBA single game 3-point record. How did he do this? He had a crushing shooting night the game before, missing all his 3s. Mortals like you and me would've been shy out there on the court again, second-guessing whether to take a three-point shot ever again. Not Stephen. He did a 180 and went from zero to hero.

Expect many bad days in your life and for them to be memorable

By the time you reach the age of 35, you will have lived on planet earth almost 13,000 days. There is no escaping having multiple bad days in your life, meaning, you're bound to have them. One of the worst days of my life took place in my late 20s. My cousin in San Diego, CA invited me to her birthday party at her apartment. There was alcohol and I drank several drinks. I waited about an hour after my last drink to leave the party; it was late, and I had to drive north to my home in Oceanside, about a 40-minute drive. While on Interstate Highway 5, I started dozing off. Instead of pulling over and resting, I kept driving.

I can still see the scary image of my car accelerating toward the back of a pick-up truck, and hitting it. The sight has been burned in my memory. Apparently, I had dozed off once again for a few seconds, and my foot had come down hard on the accelerator. I woke up just before hitting the vehicle in front, slammed my brakes, but it was too late. The pick-up pulled over to the shoulder, and I followed. My mind was racing. All I could think of was whether or not I had hurt the passengers of the pick-up. Two ladies walked out and one of them was pretty livid with me. I apologized to them for hitting their vehicle, and asked if they were okay. I explained to them that I had fallen asleep at the wheel. One of the ladies looked at the back bumper of the truck, and finding no visible damage, told her companion everything was okay and to get back inside. They drove off.

When I got home, I looked at the front of my car. It had sustained considerable damage. My radiator had busted and fluid was leaking. More importantly, I was so disappointed in myself. I could've killed someone! I spent many days after this event thinking how lucky I'd been to not have seriously injured those passengers. How I had been fortunate to avoid a collision big enough to warrant medical responders on scene or police involvement. This could've ruined my career and set me back many years.

Beating myself up in my mind for what had happened on the freeway the night of my cousin's birthday wasn't helping me in any way. I felt a change in me was necessary. I pledged to never drink more than one alcoholic beverage without a designated driver and to never drink any alcohol after 9 p.m. If I did drink one alcoholic beverage during an outing, I also vowed to drink an entire cup of water slowly before driving away from any premises. See, you have to make promises to yourself that are realistic and that you can maintain. I know I'll always have social outings in my life where alcohol will be available. I would no doubt break a promise to never drink alcohol again. My best option then was to limit myself in such a way that would allow me to drink responsibly. I have not broken my rules to this day.

You will always remember the bad days in your life. Our brains are wired to burn these bad events in our memories so that we can avoid doing them again in the future. But our brains are not hard wired to move us past these moments of poor performance or judgment. We have to consciously spend energy convincing ourselves that we can be better, and provided no one died or you didn't end up in jail, you can bounce back from crappy days as soon as you want to. Practice the 180 Exercise from above after every bad day and you'll one day become an elite performer in whatever life challenge comes your way. Setbacks will become bounce-backs sooner than normal, and you will be admired for both your optimism and resilience. Be like a spring and remember the old adage: What doesn't kill you can only make you stronger!

Chapter 15 Main Points:
1. Your mistakes or failures don't have to define who you are. Having bad days is a part of life.
2. Having bad days give you the opportunity to practice the art of 180. The more you practice purposely forgetting or putting behind you, your poor performances, the better you will get at bouncing back swiftly.
3. Our brain works against us, making us remember our poor performances more than our good ones. Therefore, to become a great performer in any thing you decide to do with your life, you'll need to think, live, and breath the concept of 180.

Notes

Chapter 1: Understanding White People & Avoiding Ignorance

I recently read an article online: "Students of all races prefer teachers of color, Finds NYU Steinhardt study," NYU.edu, October 5, 2016, https://www.nyu.edu/about/news-publications/news/2016/october/students-of-all-races-prefer-teachers-of-color--finds-nyu-steinh.html

Chapter 3: Check Your Expectations & Take Profitable Action

On his blog: "Success through goal setting, part 1 of 3," Briantracy.com, http://www.briantracy.com/blog/personal-success/success-through-goal-setting-part-1-of-3/

Chapter 4: Write Goals Down & Expect Positive Outcomes

On his blog: "The formula that puts you in control of success," Jackcanfield.com, http://jackcanfield.com/blog/the-formula-that-puts-you-in-control-of-success/

In 2007, Dr. Gail Matthews: "Study focuses on strategies for achieving goals, resolutions," Dominican.edu, http://www.dominican.edu/dominicannews/study-highlights-strategies-for-achieving-goals

Chapter 9: You're Right, School Does Suck

Last time I checked: "10 worst paying college majors," Forbes.com, November 27, 2014, by James Marshall Crotty, https://www.forbes.com/sites/jamesmarshallcrotty/2014/11/27/10-worst-paying-college-majors/2/

According to the National Assessment of Educational Progress: "High school seniors aren't college ready," USNews.com, April 27, 2016, by Lauren Camera, https://www.usnews.com/news/articles/2016-04-27/high-school-seniors-arent-college-ready-naep-data-show

Chapter 12: Skip Going to A Four-Year University After High Scholl

Universities have taken advantage: "The real reason college tuition costs so much," NYTimes.com, April 4, 2015, by Paul F. Campos, https://www.nytimes.com/2015/04/05/opinion/sunday/the-real-reason-college-tuition-costs-so-much.html?_r=0

A January 2016 report: "Gateway to higher ed? A TC report ranks states on rates of student transfer to four-year universities and completion of bachelor's degrees," TC.Columbia.edu,

http://www.tc.columbia.edu/articles/2016/januar
y/gateway-to-higher-ed-a-tc-report-ranks-
states-on-rates-of-student-transfer-to-f/

About The Author

C. (Carlos) Osvaldo Gomez was born in Delicias, Chihuahua, Mexico in 1976. In 1983, he immigrated to the United States with his mother and older sister, residing in San Jose, CA. After gaining residency status, he attended San Jose City College and then transferred to UC Santa Barbara, majoring in Biological Sciences. He earned a teaching credential and Masters in Education also from UC Santa Barbara. He taught in San Jose CA, and returned to graduate school, earning a Masters in Administration and Leadership. He became a high school Assistant Principal at the age of 28 and worked as a school administrator for 10 years before returning back to teaching in 2015.

C. Osvaldo Gomez has been featured in the San Diego Union Tribune for his work as an Assistant Principal and helping troubled teens. His students call him: Homie G because "he's like a homie." He's also been featured on Money Magazine with his wife and children for having amassed over a million dollars in net worth before 40 years of age. He is a freelance blogger, writing online educational articles. He's also a personal finance blogger at www.commoncoremoney.com. To continue helping teens, especially outside of school, C. Osvaldo Gomez started a YouTube channel and the website, www.cosvaldogomez.com.

C. Osvaldo Gomez is no stranger to writing, having been published online and in anthologies in the short fiction genre. He considers starting a family as his greatest achievement.

Made in the USA
Coppell, TX
06 February 2022

73057150R00100